GENE HOVIS'S
UPTOWN DOWN HOME
COOKBOOK

by

Gene Hovis with Sylvia Rosenthal

REBUS   New York

For information about ordering this book, or about permission to reproduce selections
from this book, write to HOTECO, Inc., 524 Warren Street, Hudson, New York 12534.

Library of Congress Cataloging-in-Publication Data

Hovis, Gene
(Uptown down home cookbook)
Gene Hovis's uptown down home cookbook / by Gene Hovis with Sylvia Rosenthal.
p.   cm.
Originally published: Boston : Little Brown, c1987.
Includes index.
ISBN 0-929661-15-X
1. Cookery, American—Southern style. I. Rosenthal, Sylvia Dworsky, 1911-
II. Title. III. Title: Uptown down home cookbook.
TX715H8385   1993
641.5975—dc20   93-30007
CIP

HAL

Designed by Jeanne Abboud

Published by Rebus, Inc. • New York

PRINTED IN THE UNITED STATES OF AMERICA
10 9 8 7 6 5 4 3 2

For Mama and Hans

Acknowledgments

I wish to thank my family and friends for their enthusiastic support and encouragement during this book's period of gestation, with a special word of appreciation for their cooperation and willingness at all times to taste, eat, and advise. My warmest thanks to Angela, Anne, Bill, Bobbie, Brooke, Doris, Eleanor, Elizabetta, Ernst, Frank, Gerrard, Gilbert, Gordon, Gray, Harriette, the Holleriths, Hy, Jerry, Joel, John, Leo, Lin, Lloyd, Lorraine, Ma Bert, Melba, Michael, Nevada Meat Market, Niall, Nico, Peter, Ponchitta, Richard, Robert, Sisi, and the Young sisters.

I want, also, to express my heartfelt appreciation to Genevieve Young for her sage advice and guidance and to Ray Roberts, my editor, for his help, counsel, and unfailing good humor.

Gene Hovis

Contents

[handwritten annotation next to SOUPS: pg. 46, 51 ✳]

Foreword

⊠ We might think of this book as a kind of gastronomic reminiscence that begins a long time ago in a small town in North Carolina. Looming large on the landscape is a wood-burning stove in a kitchen presided over by my grandmother, a lady with a discriminating palate and limitless creativity whom you will meet later on.

Food and eating it were a serious business in that household. My mother, my aunts, and even my godmother were talented and enthusiastic cooks. Every occasion, from a funeral to a wedding, was observed with a food-heaped groaning board, the presence of which blunted the edge of sadness or sent the spirit of a happy time soaring.

A great deal of time, energy, and talk were devoted to the subject of food. We discussed it before we ate, while we were eating, and after we finished. It was then that I had my first cooking lessons, subliminal though they were, for at the time I was aware only of my fascination with the graceful and seemingly effortless trimming, chopping, mixing, stirring, and tasting (*much* tasting and more talk) that preceded the completion of each dish.

The cooking was straightforward and basic. No nonsense. No gimmicks. Only the best and freshest ingredients were acceptable, each brought to the peak of its flavor with appropriate cooking techniques. Fussy, pretentious food was frowned on. The desired goal was food that was disarmingly simple and honest in which the taste of each ingredient was highlighted. This has been my guiding principle throughout my professional cooking career and is the theme for the recipes in this book. Although my cooking style is understandably rooted in the tradition of American southern cooking, over the years I have borrowed and adapted a bit here and there from other cuisines. Fashions in food are as trendy and changeable as women's hemlines and men's lapels, but simple, delicious food will never go out of style.

I have assembled in this volume recipes that I and my friends have enjoyed. One of my great pleasures is entertaining at home, particularly at small, informal dinners. I can't think of a better way to please ourselves and our friends. Restaurant dining is not in the same league, even ignoring the astronomical cost of eating at good restaurants. Dining at home is more comfortable and can be just as delicious, if not more so.

The recipes in this book offer a wide range of choices with many simple but impressive dishes that can be prepared well in advance. With sensible planning, you can entertain without spending long hours in the kitchen, although that may occasionally have its advantages. A kitchen can be a haven where you can flush out anxieties and beat annoyances into oblivion in a flurry of kneading, chopping, or mixing. However, if you organize thoughtfully, you can present a fine dinner and still meet your guests feeling relaxed and not harried.

Try to think of recipes as an incentive and general guide rather than as a rigid formula to be followed slavishly. Every time you cook, you can bring a bit of individuality and spontaneity to the dish. No recipe is ever really final. Some fine discoveries have been made when a resourceful cook ran out of an ingredient and had to scurry around for something to take its place. You have only to consider some of the great recipes that, like folk songs, have traveled around the world absorbing different nuances of flavors to appreciate that there is indeed more than one way to prepare a dish.

Get involved with your materials when you cook, just as gardeners and painters must do. Smell, feel, and taste the ingredients. Tasting is one of the pleasures and imperatives of cooking. Ingredients vary: some lemons are sourer than others; the tomatoes may be more or less acid than the ones you used previously. Individual tastes also vary, and the exact amount of seasonings can be decided only by the cook, who is in the best position to know what will please the diners.

Keep in mind that good food begins at the market with careful selection of ingredients. Cooking a tired, limp vegetable is unlikely to improve it unless it ends up in the soup pot. If the string beans don't snap when bent in half, take a look at the broccoli. If the veal resembles beef, think about chicken. Don't settle for second best. True elegance in food stems from first-rate ingredients carefully prepared.

I do hope you will find this book helpful and that you will enjoy it as much as I have in bringing it to you.

Gene Hovis

GENE HOVIS'S
UPTOWN DOWN HOME
COOKBOOK

Granny Dameron

Mary Cooper Dameron — Granny Dameron — was my maternal grandmother. She was born in the mid-1800s in North Carolina, the daughter of slaves. Very early she was taken into the home of a British-born family named Cooper. As a young child, she worked in the fields, planting, tending, and harvesting the crops. She later became the cook in the Cooper household, where she learned to read, but she was never taught to write. She married George Dameron, and together they had seven children. She was widowed early and raised her family alone.

Our visits to Granny Dameron's home loom large in my memory: hot summer nights when we gathered on her front porch, drinking lemonade and guzzling her delicious cookies while she regaled us with fascinating stories about her life. There was no television at that time, but her reminiscences were as riveting and entertaining for us as any blockbuster movie enjoyed by young people today.

Granny Dameron was tall and thin, with a quiet dignity and great elegance. After my grandfather's death, she always wore black dresses relieved by a dazzlingly white, starched apron. On Sundays she added a white lace collar to the neck of her dress. Her speech was a curious blend of a soft southern drawl and British expressions and intonations picked up from the Coopers. Granny Dameron never *set* the table: she *laid* it. She grew to-MAH-toes and "Arsh" (Irish) potatoes; she made sandwiches from loaf bread (white bread).

She was a superb cook and a fabulous seamstress. As a child, I thought that Granny Dameron must be quite rich. Her dining room table, always covered with a lovely hand-crocheted cloth and pretty hand-embroidered napkins, a bowl of fresh flowers in the center, looked opulent and lavish. It would be laden with watermelon pickles, chow-chow (cabbage relish), pickled beets, stuffed baked chickens, an assortment of fresh cooked vegetables, hot yeast pocketbook rolls, a towering, snowy coconut cake with a filling of homemade jam, and in the summer, delicious lemonade, rich creamy ice cream, and as much iced tea as we could hold. It wasn't until I reached my teens that I realized that very little of this opulence represented an outlay of actual cash, since there was a limited supply of that commodity in Granny Dameron's life. She herself raised on her own land practically everything she served. Granny Dameron had no room in her life for idleness or waste.

We children frequently pestered Granny Dameron for coffee, a request that she steadfastly refused. One day, one of us — I forget who — thought to say, "Why not? Why can't we have some coffee?"

"Because it will make you black," replied Granny with a perfectly straight face.

For some peculiar reason, the absurdity of the answer put an end to our coffee demands, for a while anyway.

Wednesday afternoon was Granny Dameron's day at home. Few people in those times had telephones, but Granny Dameron was sure that between three and five people, mostly her church ladies, all of whom seemed to be widowed, would drop by each week. She always had a supply of freshly baked pies and cakes awaiting the unannounced guests. This was the era when children were supposed to be seen and not heard, and it was clear that Granny Dameron considered her conversations with her friends too adult for us small fry to participate in. I loved helping with the serving because it gave me the opportunity to eavesdrop on the drama and intrigue of the grown-up world. In retrospect, the drama and intrigue were some warmed over, innocuous church gossip, a few opinions about how the preacher was behaving, and considerable time and effort given over to a discussion of recipes and what should be served at the next camp meeting. But at the time, I felt as if I were privy to a series of dramatic situations, pulsating with all kinds of grown-up, mysterious happenings.

You were never hungry when you left Granny Dameron's house, but to make doubly sure that such a calamity would not befall us, each of us went home with a substantial Care package from Granny's kitchen.

Appetizers
and
Hors d'Oeuvres

Appetizers and Hors d'Oeuvres

The predinner period when your guests are in the process of arriving, exchanging greetings, and beginning to relax can set the scene for a convivial evening. The presence of some tasty, interesting morsels and the usual drinks will start the gastric juices perking, although I have noticed that, given the stimulation of other guests and a party atmosphere, tomato juice with or without vodka, or tonic water with or without gin, is often equally effective.

In the pages that follow, you will find a variety of delicious little tidbits, some hot, some cold, to whet appetites for dinner, serve as a first course, or keep your guests pleasantly occupied at cocktail parties, receptions, or teas. Many can be prepared well in advance of serving, requiring only a brief interlude in the oven to be completed. Often I serve a variety of hors d'oeuvres substantial enough to substitute for a first course at the table, thereby making life easier for the cook. A sit-down or buffet luncheon consisting exclusively of many different hors d'oeuvres is always well received.

The appetizing array of raw vegetables that has preceded so many dinners seems to have lost its popularity recently, but I have no intention of abandoning it. Nature paints her produce with a dazzling range of colors, and what can be more tempting than a platter heaped with verdant broccoli or snowy cauliflower flowerets, red and white radishes, celery and carrot sticks, rounds of yellow and green squash, fresh mushrooms, and the like? (What is not devoured can be transformed into the next day's soup or vegetables vinaigrette on a bed of crisp lettuce.) Accompany the vegetables with a dip, such as mayonnaise mixed with a bit of curry powder; sour cream sparked with mashed anchovies, chopped parsley, and shallots; a small bowl of plain celery salt; a mixture of mayonnaise and sour cream with a dash of Dijon mustard and chopped shallots; or any savory combination that appeals to you.

⬚ Asparagus Rolls

1 cup grated sharp cheddar cheese
1/8 pound (1/2 stick) butter
24 thin asparagus stalks

cayenne pepper
24 slices white bread
1/4 pound (1 stick) butter, melted

1. Place grated cheese and butter in a small bowl, cover, and leave out of the refrigerator for 5 or 6 hours, or overnight.
2. Steam asparagus until tender. Drain and cool.
3. Mash cheese and butter together to form a thick, smooth paste. Add a few dashes of cayenne pepper, to taste.
4. Trim crusts from bread and flatten slices with a rolling pin.
5. Spread each slice of bread with a generous teaspoon of the cheese-butter mixture.
6. Place an asparagus spear on the bottom of each slice and roll tightly. Trim away any of the asparagus stem that protrudes from the end.
7. Place rolls seam side down on a baking sheet.
8. Brush each roll with melted butter. Refrigerate until ready to use.
9. Preheat broiler. Place rolls 3 inches under broiler heat. Watch carefully to avoid burning, and broil until golden brown. Turn and brown other side. Serve hot. Rolls may be served whole or cut in half.

⬚ Avocado-Lime Dip

SERVES 6 TO 8

3 ripe avocados
1 tablespoon grated lime rind
1/4 cup lime juice
1/4 cup finely chopped red onion
2 cloves garlic, finely minced
1/4 cup finely chopped green pepper

1/4 cup finely chopped red pepper
1/4 cup finely minced fresh parsley
1 tablespoon tequila
dash of Tabasco sauce
salt

1. Peel avocados, cut into chunks, and place in container of food processor, using the steel blade. Puree with a few off-and-on turns until smooth.

2. Scrape puree into a bowl and add lime rind and lime juice.

3. Add chopped onion, garlic, peppers, and parsley, and mix well.

4. Add tequila, Tabasco sauce, and salt to taste. Taste and adjust seasoning.

5. Place in a small serving bowl and cover with plastic wrap. Chill in refrigerator until serving time.

6. Serve with buttered melba toast rounds or taco chips.

⊠ Avocado Mousse with Shrimp

A fine appetizer, or hot-weather luncheon or supper dish. You might also consider filling the center with crabmeat, or on a less costly scale you could use cherry tomatoes, watercress, or Belgian endive, either alone or in combination.

SERVES 8 OR MORE AS APPETIZER,
4 AS MAIN COURSE

3 medium-size, very ripe avocados
1/4 cup chopped fresh dill
1/4 cup chopped watercress
1 tablespoon chopped shallots
juice of 1 lemon
1/4 cup dry white wine
1/4 cup water

2 packages unflavored gelatin
1/2 cup sour cream
salt and freshly ground pepper
1 cup heavy cream, whipped
1 cup boiled shrimp or crabmeat
mustard mayonnaise (below)

1. Oil a 4-cup ring mold and set aside.

2. Peel avocados and cut into chunks. Place in container of food processor, using the steel blade. Add dill, watercress, shallots, and lemon juice, and blend until smooth. You will have about 2 cups.

3. Combine white wine and water in a small heatproof bowl. Sprinkle gelatin over liquid and let soften. When soft, heat gently, stirring, until granules are dissolved.

4. Add dissolved gelatin to avocado mixture in processor and blend for a few seconds.

5. Add sour cream and blend until completely smooth.

6. Transfer to a bowl and add salt and pepper to taste.

7. Whip cream until it mounds softly. Do not overbeat.

8. Remove puree from refrigerator and fold in whipped cream.

9. Transfer mixture to the prepared ring mold and smooth top with a spatula. Cover with plastic wrap, and refrigerate for 4 to 6 hours or overnight.

10. Unmold (page 29) on a chilled round platter. Fill center with boiled shrimp or crabmeat and serve with mustard mayonnaise sauce.

Mustard Mayonnaise

²/₃ *cup mayonnaise*
2 tablespoons Dijon mustard
1 teaspoon lemon juice

1 teaspoon vodka
1 tablespoon finely chopped shallots

Combine all ingredients in a small bowl and blend well.

▨ Glazed Bacon Crisps

These were one of Granny Dameron's specialties, and good they are. They generally evoke "oh's" and "ah's" with a request for more.

SERVES 8

¹/₂ pound sliced bacon at room
   *temperature**
1 cup dark brown sugar

1. Preheat oven to 250°.

2. Dredge both sides of bacon slices generously with brown sugar, patting it to make it stick.

3. Place slices on a flat baking sheet in a single layer, without overlapping. Bake for 30 to 40 minutes, until crisp.

4. Remove strips from pan and drain on brown paper.

5. When cool, break each slice in half and arrange on a silver or glass serving platter.

*If bacon has not been brought to room temperature, you can speed up the warming process by putting slices in a 250° oven for a few minutes until they lose their cool and soften slightly.

⊠ Beet Ring with Shrimp

An appetizer course that can also serve as a summer lunch or supper.

SERVES 6

2 pounds fresh beets
salt
1¹/₂ tablespoons unflavored gelatin
¹/₃ cup cold water
2 tablespoons (or more) prepared
*   horseradish*

3 tablespoons dark brown sugar
2 tablespoons sherry wine vinegar
salt and freshly ground pepper
1 pound cooked shrimp, shelled and
*   deveined*
watercress and endive

SAUCE
1 cup shallot-seasoned mayonnaise
*   (page 161)*
¹/₂ cup chili sauce

1 teaspoon Worcestershire sauce
1 tablespoon lemon juice

1. Oil a 4-cup ring mold and set aside.
2. Scrub beets, remove tops, place in a pot, and cover with lightly salted water. Bring to a boil, lower heat, and simmer, covered, until beets are fork tender. (They can take anywhere from 30 minutes to 1 hour, depending on size and freshness.)
3. Sprinkle gelatin over cold water and let soften.
4. When beets are tender, remove from pot, reserving liquid. Peel beets when cool.
5. Strain beet liquid through a few thicknesses of cheesecloth. Place 2 cups beet liquid in the pot, add softened gelatin, and stir over low heat until gelatin is dissolved and liquid is clear. Mix in horseradish, brown sugar, vinegar, and salt and pepper to taste.
6. Chop the beets moderately fine, fold into the liquid, and taste and correct seasoning. You may want to add more horseradish.
7. Pour into the oiled mold and refrigerate for several hours or overnight.
8. Mix together all the sauce ingredients and set aside.
9. When ready to serve, unmold (page 29) on chilled round platter. Garnish with watercress and endive. Place cooked shrimp in the center of the ring. Pass sauce separately.

⊠ Caviar on Fried Toast

My mother often rewarded good behavior when we were small with her special fried bread topped with a thick layer of her home-made, fruit-laden jam. I have taken a few liberties with her for-mula, such as omitting the jam and substituting sour cream studded with finely chopped shallots and crowned with caviar. For an hors d'oeuvre, I use small rounds of bread; for an appetizer, large rounds 3 inches or more.

SERVES 6

¹/₄ cup sour cream
2 tablespoons finely chopped shallots
¹/₃ cup mayonnaise
1 tablespoon vodka
¹/₂ teaspoon lemon juice
white pepper

6 slices white bread
¹/₄ pound (1 stick) unsalted butter
4 ounces caviar
2 hard-cooked eggs
lemon wedges

1. In a small bowl, combine sour cream, shallots, mayonnaise, vodka, lemon juice, and pepper. Blend well and refrigerate for 2 or 3 hours.

2. Cut 6 large bread rounds.

3. Melt butter in a large skillet. When hot, add bread rounds and sauté on both sides until golden and crisp. Set aside.

4. Spread tops of toast rounds with cream-mayonnaise mixture. Cover with a generous serving of caviar.

5. Separate hard-cooked egg whites and egg yolks. Force each separately through a strainer.

6. Sprinkle outside borders of toast rounds with egg white and place a circle of yolks in the center.

7. Serve on glass salad plates and garnish with lemon wedges.

⊠ Roquefort Cheese Cornucopias

If you have access to a food store that specializes in Hungarian products, do buy Paprikash salami for this piquant little tidbit; otherwise, you can use regular salami.

MAKES 24 PIECES

¹/₄ pound Roquefort cheese, crumbled
3-ounce cake of cream cheese
2 tablespoons chopped parsley or
chives

freshly ground pepper
24 thin slices salami, Paprikash or
regular

1. Combine crumbled Roquefort cheese and cream cheese until well blended.
2. Blend in chopped parsley or chives and pepper to taste.
3. Fold salami slices in half, then in quarters. Secure closed the folded edges of the triangle with a toothpick. Spread open to make a cornucopia.
4. Fill cornucopias with cheese mixture. For a professional look, use a pastry tube with a large star opening to insert the filling.
5. Refrigerate until serving time.

⊠ Barbecued Chicken Wings

These are frequently requested by my guests. I pile the wings high on a platter garnished with parsley sprigs and accompany them with lots of paper napkins.

SERVES 10 TO 12

20 small chicken wings
¹/₂ cup whole wheat flour
1 tablespoon paprika

salt and freshly ground pepper
barbecue sauce (page 94)

1. Butter a large baking sheet. Preheat oven to 400°.
2. Wash wings and wipe dry. Trim away wing tips and divide wings in two at the joint.
3. Combine flour, paprika, salt, and pepper.
4. Dust wings lightly with flour mixture and arrange on baking sheet.
5. Bake in preheated oven for 20 minutes.
6. Drain off any fat that has accumulated on baking sheet. Spoon barbecue sauce over wings.
7. Return wings to oven and continue baking, basting frequently, for 25 to 30 minutes longer, or until done. Remove from oven and let cool briefly before serving.

▨ Miniature Chicken and Mushroom Turnovers

A delicious filling encased in bite-sized, half-moon-shaped, flaky pastry, served hot.

MAKES ABOUT 16

2 tablespoons butter
1/2 cup finely chopped mushrooms
1 small onion, finely chopped
2 cups finely chopped cooked chicken

1/2 cup béchamel sauce (page 159)
salt and freshly ground pepper
cream cheese pastry (below)

1. Preheat oven to 350°.
2. Heat butter in a small skillet and sauté mushrooms and onions until onions are wilted and liquid is evaporated.
3. Place chopped chicken in a bowl and combine with mushrooms and onions.
4. Add 1/2 cup béchamel sauce, or enough to bind ingredients together. Taste and add salt and pepper if needed.
5. Roll out pastry on a lightly floured surface. Cut into 2- or 2 1/2-inch rounds with a biscuit cutter. Gather up unused bits of dough and roll out again for more rounds.
6. Place a small mound of chicken mixture in the center of each round and fold in half. With the tines of a fork, press around the outside border to seal tightly. Prick top lightly.
7. Transfer turnovers to a lightly oiled cookie sheet.
8. Bake 10 to 15 minutes until light biscuit color. Serve hot.

Cream Cheese Pastry

1/2 pound cream cheese at room temperature
2 cups sifted flour

1/2 pound butter at room temperature

Blend together cream cheese and butter. Mix in flour until well combined. Form into a ball and flatten slightly. Cover with plastic wrap and chill in refrigerator for a few hours or overnight. Let come to room temperature before rolling out. Unused dough can be refrigerated or frozen for later use.

Ham Crescents: Roll out cream cheese pastry into a large rectangle. Cover with Virginia ham, sliced paper-thin. Spread lightly with Dijon mustard. With cookie cutter, cut out rounds of ham-covered pastry and proceed as above. Serve hot.

▨ Clam Fritters

Make these in the morning, refrigerate them, and deep-fry quickly at serving time.

MAKES ABOUT 30

1 cup minced clams, fresh or canned, well drained
2 tablespoons finely chopped shallots
2 tablespoons finely chopped fresh parsley
1 egg, beaten
2 to 3 tablespoons fine bread crumbs

salt and freshly ground pepper
generous dash of hot pepper sauce
1/2 cup flour
2 eggs, well beaten
1 cup fine bread crumbs
oil

1. Combine clams, shallots, parsley, egg, and sufficient bread crumbs to bind mixture together.
2. Mix in salt, pepper, and hot pepper sauce to taste.
3. Form into small patties the size of a quarter.
4. Place flour on a square of wax paper. Beat eggs in a flat, shallow bowl. Spread bread crumbs on another square of wax paper, a small amount at a time so as not to dampen all the crumbs.
5. Dredge patties in flour, dip in beaten egg, allowing the excess to drip back in the bowl. Coat with bread crumbs.
6. Place on a baking sheet lined with wax paper and refrigerate.
7. At serving time, heat 3 inches of oil in a deep skillet or deep fat fryer.
8. Fry until golden, 5 to 8 minutes, turning once. Do not crowd; you may have to do them in batches. Drain on brown paper. Serve with lemon wedges or tartar sauce (page 160).

▨ Deviled Crab

Served in tiny scallop shells, this makes a superb hors d'oeuvre, and in larger shells, a fine main course.

SERVES 14 TO 16 AS APPETIZER,
4 AS MAIN COURSE

1 pound lump crabmeat
4 tablespoons (¹/₂ stick) butter
2 tablespoons finely chopped onion
2 tablespoons finely chopped celery
¹/₂ cup mayonnaise
¹/₂ cup freshly grated Parmesan
  cheese

1 tablespoon finely chopped parsley
1 teaspoon fresh lemon juice
1 teaspoon dry sherry
1 teaspoon freshly ground pepper
Tabasco sauce

TOPPING
2 tablespoons mayonnaise
1 tablespoon freshly grated Parmesan
  cheese

1. Pick over crabmeat to remove cartilage and bone. Treat it gently so as not to break up the lumps. Place crab in a mixing bowl.

2. Heat butter in a small skillet and add onion and celery. Cook until wilted. Set aside to cool.

3. Preheat the broiler.

4. Add onion and celery mixture, mayonnaise, and grated cheese to the crabmeat. Add parsley, lemon juice, sherry, pepper, and a few squirts of Tabasco. Blend gently so as not to break up the lumps. Taste for seasoning and add more Tabasco if you want it zippier.

5. If you are to serve this as an hors d'oeuvre, spoon the mixture into 14 to 16 small scallop shells. For a main course, spoon it into 4 large shells.

6. Blend topping ingredients together. Spoon equal portions of this mixture over the tops of crab and smooth it over. Place under the broiler until bubbling and golden brown. Serve hot.

▨ Cucumber-Ratatouille Rounds

A cold hors d'oeuvre that makes an attractive presentation and a perfect answer to what to serve to your vegetarian friends. Prepare the ratatouille a day or two ahead of when you plan to serve it.

MAKES ABOUT 36 ROUNDS

3 tablespoons olive oil
1 clove garlic, finely chopped
1 small onion, finely chopped
1 stalk celery, finely chopped
1 small eggplant, unskinned, finely chopped
2 ripe tomatoes, skinned, seeded, and finely chopped, or 1-pound can plum tomatoes, drained and finely chopped

2 large green olives, finely chopped
1 small zucchini, finely chopped
1 tablespoon dried oregano
¹/₄ cup minced fresh parsley
salt and freshly ground pepper
2 medium-size seedless cucumbers

1. In a medium-size saucepan, heat oil and sauté garlic, onion, and celery until wilted but not browned.

2. Add eggplant and continue sautéing until eggplant is soft and translucent.

3. Add chopped tomatoes, olives, zucchini, oregano, and parsley, and cook over low heat until thickened, stirring from time to time.

4. Taste, and add salt and pepper as needed.

5. Transfer to a bowl, cool, and cover bowl with plastic wrap. Chill in refrigerator overnight.

6. Remove ratatouille from refrigerator 1 hour before serving and let come to room temperature.

7. Scrub cucumbers and score with the tines of a fork. Cut into ¹/₄-inch rounds, place on paper towels, and refrigerate until ready to use.

8. To serve, place ¹/₂ teaspoon of ratatouille in the center of each cucumber round and arrange rounds in concentric circles on a silver or glass tray.

▨ Curried Eggs

Use small eggs; they look neat and tidy and are easier to manage than the large ones, particularly as finger food. Quail eggs are super, if you happen to have access to a quail farm. Otherwise, chicken eggs will do nicely. If you are serving them as an appetizer course, serve two halves on a bed of watercress or Bibb lettuce. As an hors d'oeuvre, they require only an attractive serving platter.

SERVES 4 TO 6

6 small hard-cooked eggs
1 tablespoon finely chopped fresh
  chives
1 tablespoon soft butter
1 tablespoon mayonnaise

1 teaspoon Dijon mustard
1 to 2 tablespoons curry powder
salt and freshly ground pepper
chopped chutney

1. Peel eggs and cut in half lengthwise. Remove yolks and place whites in a bowl of ice water to firm and brighten them.

2. Mash yolks through a sieve into a small bowl.

3. Add chives, butter, mayonnaise, and mustard, and mix well. Mix in curry powder, tasting as you go. The strength of curry powders varies, as do preferences for a little or a lot of the seasoning. Season with salt and pepper.

4. Drain egg whites on paper towels and pat dry.

5. Fill egg white cavities with yolk mixture. (A pastry tube equipped with a large star tip for this step will give the finished product a professional and stylish look.) Refrigerate until serving time.

6. Just before serving, garnish the center of each half-egg with a small lump of chopped chutney.

▨ Scotch Eggs

I first sampled Scotch eggs, courtesy of an English friend, in a lovely timeworn, wood-paneled pub in London. Scotch eggs, in case you are as unknowing as I was, are hard-cooked eggs in an overcoat of sausage meat and bread crumbs, deep-fried. They were served whole and cold, but I prefer them cut into quarters and a bit warm. I find a whole egg too large for easy handling.

SERVES 6

6 hard-cooked eggs
2½ cups fresh dry bread crumbs
1 medium onion, chopped
¼ cup minced fresh parsley

1½ pounds sausage meat
3 eggs, beaten
vegetable oil

1. Peel hard-cooked eggs and place in a bowl of cold water. Refrigerate overnight or until cold and firm.

2. Remove eggs from refrigerator, drain well, and pat dry. Cut lengthwise into quarters.

3. To make dry bread crumbs, crisp about 10 slices of bread on a baking sheet in a 250° oven. Cut the crisped bread into cubes and place in container of food processor, using the steel blade. Process until crumbs are uniformly fine. Transfer to a bowl.

4. Process chopped onion and parsley until fine.

5. Remove sausage meat from the casing and continue processing with on-and-off turns until mixture is combined. Mixture will be rather sticky. Transfer to a bowl.

6. Pat sausage mixture into small, thin patties about 3 inches in diameter. Place an egg quarter in the center of each patty and encase it in the coating.

7. Place beaten eggs in a shallow bowl. Spread bread crumbs on a square of wax paper.

8. Dip coated egg into beaten egg, letting the excess drip back into the bowl. Roll in bread crumbs.

9. Arrange eggs on a baking sheet lined with wax paper. Cover lightly with plastic wrap and refrigerate until ready to use.

10. Heat vegetable oil in a large, deep skillet until hot. Using a slotted spoon, gently tilt eggs into hot oil. Fry for 10 to 12 minutes until they become a deep golden brown. Watch carefully to make sure the oil doesn't get so hot that the eggs burn. Lower the heat if they seem to be browning too quickly.

11. As eggs are done, remove with a slotted spoon and place on absorbent paper towels to drain. Keep them warm until all are finished.

▨ Bourbon Frankfurters

Cocktail-size frankfurters may be used, but I prefer the regular-size franks, sliced.

SERVES 10 TO 12

1 pound frankfurters
12-ounce bottle chili sauce
1/2 cup dark brown sugar

2 teaspoons Worcestershire sauce
1/2 cup bourbon

1. Wipe frankfurters with a wet paper towel and slice into 1/2-inch rounds.

2. In a heavy pot with a cover, mix chili sauce, brown sugar, Worcestershire sauce, and bourbon.

3. Place sliced frankfurters in the sauce, cover pot, and cook over very low heat for 2 hours, stirring occasionally. (To avoid possibility of scorching, use a flame control device, such as an asbestos pad, over source of heat.)

4. Remove to a chafing dish and serve with toothpicks.

▨ Chicken Liver Pâté with Cognac and Pistachio Nuts

Make this a day in advance of use to give the flavors time to marry and mellow.

SERVES 8 TO 10

1 pound fresh chicken livers
1/4 cup pistachio nuts, coarsely
   chopped
1/4 pound (1 stick) butter
1 cup finely chopped small white
   onions

1/4 cup cognac
1 teaspoon port wine
salt and freshly ground pepper

1. Pick over livers and cut away connecting tissues and tabs of fat. Rinse and dry thoroughly on absorbent paper towels. It is essential that the livers be dry.

2. Spread chopped pistachio nuts in a shallow pan and heat in a 350° oven until lightly toasted, 6 to 8 minutes. Set aside when done.

3. In a large skillet, melt butter and heat until it is light brown, but do not burn. Add livers without crowding; do them in batches if your pan isn't large enough. Sauté them, shaking the pan so they cook on all sides. They should be brown on the outside but pink inside.

4. Remove livers from skillet with a slotted spoon, leaving the fat in the pan, and place livers in container of food processor.

5. Add onions to the skillet and sauté quickly until wilted.

6. Add cognac to the pan, and with a wooden spoon scrape up any brown bits adhering to bottom and sides. Bring to a boil and boil for a minute.

7. Add port wine and stir through. Add to the chicken livers.

8. Process with a few on-and-off turns until fairly fine but not pureed. There should be texture.

9. Scrape chopped liver into a bowl and fold in toasted pistachios. Add salt and pepper to taste.

10. Transfer to a small crock appropriate for serving. When completely cool, cover and refrigerate. (It may also be molded into a loaf shape, wrapped tightly in aluminum foil, and cut into slices for serving.)

11. Remove from refrigerator at least ½ hour before serving. Serve with buttered toast points.

▨ Country Liver Pâté

Recipes for pâtés are as numerous as jelly beans at Easter time, but this is one I particularly like. Pâtés are fine to have on hand for a first course or a cold lunch for unexpected guests. Refrigerated, pâtés will keep for about 10 days, but they do not freeze well. I generally serve the pâté with a bit of Cumberland sauce (below) as a garnish, but it may be omitted if you wish.

MAKES 1 LOAF

1 pound lean fresh pork, ground
1 pound salt pork, ground
1 pound pork liver
2 tablespoons butter
1 cup shallots, coarsely chopped
¾ cup half-and-half
2 eggs, lightly beaten
2 tablespoons flour

1 bay leaf, crumbled to powder
¼ cup cognac
¼ teaspoon ground cloves
½ teaspoon dried thyme
¼ teaspoon allspice
salt and pepper
¼ pound bacon

1. Preheat oven to 350°. Place baking rack in lower third of oven.

2. Combine ground fresh pork and salt pork in a large mixing bowl and keep chilled until ready to use. (I suggest that you have your butcher grind fresh pork and salt pork together.)

3. Plunge pork liver into boiling water for 10 to 15 seconds. Drain and pat dry. Cut into chunks.

4. In a small skillet, heat butter and cook shallots briefly until slightly softened, but not brown.

5. Place pork liver in container of food processor, using the steel blade, and blend until smooth. Add shallots, half-and-half, eggs, flour, powdered bay leaf, cognac, cloves, thyme, and allspice. Process with a few on-and-off turns until blended.

6. Add the pork liver mixture to the bowl of ground meats and mix well.

7. Add salt and freshly ground pepper. To taste for seasoning, sauté a small spoonful and taste. Then mix in whatever seasonings you feel are needed.

8. Plunge slices of bacon into boiling water for a few minutes to blanch. Drain and pat dry.

9. Line the bottom and sides of a loaf pan with the blanched bacon.

10. Scrape mixture into the bacon-lined pan. Cover the top with wax paper and tie to close securely. Cover top with aluminum foil.

11. Set loaf pan in a larger pan. Place in oven. Add boiling water to about halfway up the outside of the loaf pan. Add more boiling water during cooking, if needed.

12. Bake for 1½ to 2 hours. Pâté is done when it has shrunk slightly from the sides of the baking pan.

13. When pâté is done, remove loaf pan from the hot water and remove coverings. Let cool at room temperature for a few hours and chill.

14. When thoroughly chilled, unmold (page 29) pâté and wrap airtight in aluminum foil. Store in refrigerator until ready to use.

Cumberland Sauce

Also good with ham or game; may be served hot or cold.

MAKES 1 CUP

1 orange	*pinch of powdered ginger*
1 lemon	*1 teaspoon Dijon mustard*
½ cup red currant jelly	*salt*
¼ cup port wine	*dash of hot pepper sauce (optional)*

1. Peel orange and lemon as thinly as possible with a potato peeler or citrus peeler, and slice the peel into fine julienne strips. Drop the peel into a pan of boiling water for a few minutes until slightly softened. Drain well.

2. Melt currant jelly in a small saucepan.

3. Squeeze juice from the orange and lemon and add to currant jelly.

4. Add the peels, port, ginger, mustard, and salt to taste. Add a dash of hot pepper sauce if you want it a bit zippier. Simmer for a few minutes.

5. Taste for seasoning and correct.

▨ Stuffed Mushrooms

Mushrooms have a lot going for them in the world of gastronomy: they perform nobly as an hors d'oeuvre before a meal, or as a vegetable or garnish with a meal, and they can be coated with chocolate as a dessert sweet.

SERVES 8 OR MORE

24 medium-size mushrooms	*1 tablespoon chopped parsley*
3 Italian sweet sausages	*¼ cup fine dry bread crumbs*
3 tablespoons butter	*1 tablespoon dry vermouth*
¼ cup finely chopped shallots	*2 tablespoons grated Parmesan cheese*

1. Wipe mushrooms clean. Remove stems, chop finely, and set aside.

2. Remove sausages from casings and crumble.

3. In a small skillet, heat butter. Add chopped mushroom stems, shallots, and sausage meat. Sauté, stirring for 10 to 15 minutes, or until vegetables are tender.

4. Remove from heat and mix in chopped parsley, bread crumbs, and vermouth, and blend thoroughly.

5. Preheat oven to 450°.

6. Fill mushroom caps with sausage mixture, mounding it nicely.

7. Place mushroom caps on a baking sheet. Sprinkle each with Parmesan cheese. Bake for 10 to 12 minutes, until heated through. Serve hot.

▨ Onion Puffs

A delicious, bite-size bit that turns out to be more exciting than its simple ingredients would suggest. Prepare them well in advance, and keep them refrigerated until your guests arrive.

SERVES 6 TO 8

24 bread rounds, 1 to 1¹/₂ inches in
diameter
¹/₂ cup mayonnaise
5 tablespoons grated Parmesan or
locatelli cheese (if available)

2 tablespoons minced fresh parsley
6 to 8 small white onions, peeled

1. Cut bread rounds with a small cookie cutter. Place on cookie sheet and toast one side only under the broiler until lightly browned.

2. Spread the untoasted side lightly with mayonnaise.

3. Blend 4 tablespoons grated cheese with minced parsley and remaining mayonnaise.

4. Thinly slice the peeled white onions. Place a slice of onion the same size as the bread on each round.

5. Mound the mayonnaise mixture over the top of each round and sprinkle with the remaining tablespoon of cheese. Refrigerate until serving time.

6. When ready to serve, place under broiler and broil until puffy and brown. They can burn quickly, so watch them carefully. Serve hot.

▨ Barbecued Pork Rolls

A fine, zippy answer to what to do with leftover meat from a fresh ham or a loin of pork. It will also do nicely as a luncheon sandwich.

MAKES 12 TO 16 SANDWICHES

4 cups cooked pork, trimmed of fat
  and finely chopped

BARBECUE SAUCE

2 tablespoons vegetable oil
1/2 cup finely chopped small white
  onions
1/4 cup sherry wine vinegar or red
  wine vinegar
1/4 cup soy sauce
3 tablespoons Worcestershire sauce

1 tablespoon dark brown sugar
1 scant teaspoon chili powder
1 teaspoon celery seeds
1 tablespoon fresh lemon juice
dash of pepper sauce
freshly ground pepper

12 to 16 small finger rolls, heated

CHOPPED CABBAGE GARNISH

1 cup finely chopped cabbage
1 tablespoon sugar

1 tablespoon white vinegar
salt and freshly ground black pepper

1. Trim pork of fat and chop finely. Set aside.

2. In a small saucepan, heat the oil and sauté the onions until wilted.

3. Mix in remaining ingredients of barbecue sauce and cook over low heat for 15 minutes.

4. Place chopped pork in a heatproof bowl and mix with hot barbecue sauce. Keep warm.

5. Toss together chopped cabbage, sugar, vinegar, salt, and pepper.

6. Split heated finger rolls in halves. Cover bottom half with 1 teaspoon of chopped cabbage.

7. Cover with 1 generous tablespoon of barbecued pork and top with remaining halves of roll. Serve warm.

Appetizers and Hors d'Oeuvres **25**

⊠ New Potatoes with Caviar

SERVES 8 TO 10

24 tiny new red potatoes
1 tablespoon salt
1/2 cup sour cream

2 tablespoons chopped chives
freshly ground black pepper
3 to 4 ounces caviar

1. Scrub potatoes with a vegetable brush. Place in a pot, cover with salted water, cover pot, and boil until tender, 15 to 20 minutes. Don't overcook.

2. Drain cooked potatoes and return to pot. Shake the pan over low heat until they are dry. Remove from pan and let cool.

3. When potatoes are cool, cut off tops with a sharp knife and reserve.

4. Using a small melon scoop, scoop out a bit of potato, leaving most of it intact.

5. Mix together sour cream, chopped chives, and a few grinds of pepper.

6. Spoon about 1 teaspoon sour cream into each potato cavity.

7. Top with caviar. Replace tops carefully and serve.

⊠ Smoked Salmon Rolls

SERVES 4 TO 6

5 ounces cream cheese at room
   temperature
1 tablespoon finely chopped red onion

1 tablespoon chopped fresh dill
freshly ground black pepper
1/2 pound thinly sliced smoked salmon

1. In a small bowl, mash together cream cheese, onion, dill, and a few grinds of black pepper.

2. Arrange smoked salmon slices on a flat surface and spread with cream cheese mixture.

3. Roll up jelly-roll fashion. Wrap tightly in plastic wrap and refrigerate for several hours.

4. Slice chilled rolls with a sharp knife into 1-inch slices. Spear each with a toothpick or place on small rounds of melba toast. Chill until ready to serve.

▨ Smoked Salmon Mousse

A tasty, substantial hors d'oeuvre, which I serve with crisp buttered toast made from French or Italian bread (below), to accompany predinner drinks.

SERVES 8 TO 10

¹/₂ pound smoked salmon
1 shallot, finely chopped
4 tablespoons (¹/₂ stick) unsalted
*   butter, melted and cooled*
2 tablespoons chopped fresh dill

¹/₂ cup sour cream
1 tablespoon lemon juice
¹/₄ cup vodka
freshly ground pepper

1. Cut salmon slices into pieces and place in container of food processor, using the steel blade. Add shallot and process briefly with a few on-and-off turns, until pureed.

2. With the motor still running, add cooled butter in a stream through the feed tube. Add dill and process a few seconds longer.

3. Scrape salmon into a bowl and fold in sour cream, lemon juice, and vodka. Add pepper to taste.

4. Cover bowl with plastic wrap and refrigerate overnight. (On the occasions when there wasn't enough time for an overnight stay in the refrigerator, I have tucked the mousse into the freezer for 20 minutes and then transferred it to the refrigerator.)

5. Transfer mousse to a serving bowl. I like to use a small soup tureen with a cover. Let mousse stand at room temperature for an hour before serving.

6. To serve, place bowl of mousse on a serving tray and surround bowl with toast.

Buttered Melba Toast

Slice a loaf of French or Italian bread. Butter each slice. Arrange on a baking sheet and place in a 200° oven for 3 hours. The slow baking at low temperature makes the toast deliciously crisp without darkening.

▨ Deep-fried Scallops

I use the large sea scallops cut in half vertically, creating two half-moon shapes. Bay scallops, fine as they are, are too small for this preparation.

SERVES 6 AS AN HORS D'OEUVRE

vegetable oil
1 pound sea scallops
2 tablespoons lemon juice
salt and freshly ground pepper

1 cup Dijon mustard
2 tablespoons minced shallots
2 tablespoons minced parsley
1½ cups fine bread crumbs

1. In a heavy kettle, heat 3 inches of oil to 375°. (To test heat if you don't have a proper thermometer, use the bread cube method: a 1-inch cube of bread will brown in fat heated to 375° in 1 minute, as long as it takes you to count to 60.)

2. Wash scallops, cut in two, sprinkle with lemon juice, and pat dry on paper towels. Sprinkle lightly with salt and pepper.

3. In a shallow bowl, combine mustard, shallots, and parsley, and mix well. Spread bread crumbs on a square of wax paper.

4. Dip the scallops first in the mustard mixture and then coat well with bread crumbs.

5. Fry 3 to 5 minutes in hot oil, until golden brown. Remove with a slotted spoon. Serve with toothpicks.

▨ Shrimp Toast

MAKES 24 TRIANGLES

½ pound raw shrimp
2 tablespoons chopped water chestnuts
1 tablespoon finely chopped onion
1 tablespoon cornstarch

1 egg, lightly beaten
salt and freshly ground pepper
12 slices thinly sliced white bread
vegetable oil

1. Shell and devein shrimp. Chop finely. Set aside.

2. Combine water chestnuts, chopped onion, cornstarch, and egg. Mix with chopped shrimp and blend to a paste. Season with salt and pepper.

3. Trim crusts from bread and cut bread into triangles. Toast on one side.

4. Spread shrimp mixture on the toasted side. (This may be done in advance and the shrimp toast refrigerated until ready to cook.)

5. In a deep fat fryer or a deep skillet, heat 3 inches of oil to 375°. Carefully lower the slices of shrimp toast with a slotted spoon into the hot oil and fry for 2 to 3 minutes, or until golden. Do only so many as will fit at a time without crowding.

6. Remove slices to absorbent paper to drain, and continue cooking until all are done. Keep the finished slices warm and serve at once.

To Unmold Gelatin or Frozen Molds

The unmolding will be easier if the mold was lightly oiled or rinsed with cold water before being filled. Never use a hard fat or butter.

To unmold, fill a bowl that is larger than the mold with warm water. Dip the mold into the water just to the rim and hold it for a few seconds. Remove it from the water and run a thin knife carefully around the edge. This breaks the air seal that is holding the gelatin to the mold. Place a large, flat plate over the top of the mold; hold the plate firmly and invert. Shake gently, holding the serving dish tightly to the mold. The mold should lift off easily. If it doesn't, cover the mold with a hot, damp towel and let it sit for a few minutes.

Train Lunches and Munches

The rumble of train wheels and the ear-piercing toot of a train whistle still evoke for me a flood of memories of Lucullan feasts neatly done up in shoe boxes. My father worked for the Southern Railway, a generous and paternal company that gave its employees and their families the spectacular perk of train passes, anywhere, anytime. The Hovis clan was not one to take this gratuity lightly, what with a favorite uncle in New Jersey and an assortment of hospitable relatives in and around New York City, even though visiting them meant a long overnight train trip from our home in North Carolina.

With the expertise of an army sergeant taking his troops on maneuvers, my resourceful and intrepid mother met the challenge of keeping her brood of four small children — each with the appetite of a voracious puppy — happy and replete during the lengthy expedition. We boarded the train with our luggage and my mother's shoe boxes. The first was opened shortly after we left the station. It was packed to overflowing with tea sandwiches of ham salad, pimiento cheese studded with chopped green olives, watercress and cream cheese, chicken salad, and chopped egg and bacon with mayonnaise. There were deviled eggs, homemade pickled beets with hard-boiled eggs, and fried chicken wings cut in two pieces. The chicken wings earned their right to inclusion in the shoe box because they were plentiful, delicious, and easy to eat, and had the added virtue of being cheap. This last was an important consideration, for my mother was not frugal by choice.

I recall the ride through Virginia as interminable and boring, but finally came the morning shortly before we arrived in Washington, D.C. That was the time for the shoe box labeled "Breakfast." Baked ham biscuits, stickies, and fruit kept our bodies and souls together as we transferred to the Pennsylvania line. I always thrilled at walking through Union Station, with its graceful Gothic arches. The station seemed to me as awesome and imposing as a museum or a cathedral.

The change of trains spelled the end of the shoe boxes. They were replaced by a truly major eating experience, for the previously out-of-bounds dining car territory was now open to us. We became surrounded by attentive waiters, snowy table linens, and a mind-boggling choice of wonderful things to eat. Were they as fabulous as I remember? I wonder. On each table were bowls of corn relish, pickles, and olives. The menu blazed with New England clam chowder, crab cakes, chicken pot pies, T-bone and porterhouse steaks, and Maryland fried chicken, among other delicacies. And such desserts! Apple dumplings with vanilla sauce, bread and butter pudding, rich creamy Philadelphia ice cream, and all manner of cakes — pound cake, devil's food, caramel cake with thick caramel icing. My favorite was banana pudding awash with whipped cream.

To this day, trains and dining cars never cease to beguile me, although the passage of time may have buffed away some of the joyful anticipation and glamour. Just a little — not much.

Sandwiches,
Plain
and
Fancy

Sandwiches, Plain and Fancy

A gathering of friends over a cup of tea or coffee, with substance provided by good-looking, good-tasting little tea sandwiches and some simple cake, is a graceful and hospitable way of entertaining, one that is not too taxing for the party-giver. Coming at the end of what might be a working day for many, teatime can be an occasion for reviving flagging spirits with socializing and delectable things to eat.

Granny Dameron had a special way with finger sandwiches that I hope to share with you. The fillings were always delicate and subtly flavored, the bread moist, and the finished product a treat for the eyes as well as the mouth. With a few simple guidelines, you will find them easy to prepare and always successful.

Utensils: You will need a very sharp knife, two small spatulas or spreaders, a cutting board, and dampened tea towels. I still use tea towels — force of habit, I suppose — but dampened paper towels will serve the same purpose, which is to keep the bread from drying out. A dried-out tea sandwich is a sorry thing.

Most fillings for the sandwiches can be made well in advance of use. Refrigerate them in small plastic containers with tight-fitting lids, labeled with contents. The seasoned butters that you will use can be stored in the same way, and they're wonderfully convenient to have on hand for sparking up vegetables, broiled meats, poultry, or fish.

Bread: Granny Dameron baked her own bread and sliced it thin-thin, but I find the commercial thinly sliced bread available in supermarkets most acceptable. It is labeled "very thin" and is available in both white and whole wheat. Both light and dark breads on a sandwich platter provide interesting color contrast and make for an attractive presentation. The recipes that follow make precise recommendations for which bread to use, but you are free to follow your own inclinations.

Refrigerate the bread before starting the sandwiches. If the bread is cold, you will have a neater, sharper edge with no ragged borders when you trim the crusts. Wipe the knife clean each time you use it.

Fillings: Sandwich mixtures should be at room temperature for easy spreading. Fillings should be light and delicate in flavor, not overseasoned. To hold bread and filling together snugly, spread the facing slices of the sandwich with soft seasoned butter, mustard mayonnaise with a dollop of finely chopped shallots, cheddar cheese minced with pimiento, or plain whipped butter.

Seasoned butter may be made with watercress, parsley, or dill. Wash the greens, discarding the coarse stems, and dry thoroughly. Moisture left on the greens will make the butter watery. You will need about one-half bunch of the greens to ½ pound (2 sticks) butter. Place in container of food processor and process with a few on-and-off turns until well combined. Let soften at room temperature before using.

Storage: Sandwiches may be made ahead of time and refrigerated, covered with damp, not wet, linen or paper toweling. Wet toweling will make the sandwiches soggy instead of moist. Remove from the refrigerator 30 minutes to an hour before serving, but leave covered with damp toweling until serving time.

The finished sandwich platters may also be arranged in advance. Cover with damp toweling and refrigerate. The important consideration is that the sandwiches not be allowed to dry out.

If you are planning the sandwiches for a picnic or a trip, pack them in storage pans — I use an aluminum lasagna pan — each layer of sandwiches labeled and covered with damp toweling.

▨ Curried Egg Sandwiches

Egg salad sandwiches with a different look.

MAKES 12 SANDWICHES

6 hard-cooked eggs
2½ tablespoons mayonnaise
1 teaspoon Dijon mustard
1 teaspoon curry powder, or to taste
1 teaspoon finely chopped shallots

salt and freshly ground pepper
12 slices thinly sliced bread, white or
    whole wheat, or 6 of each
soft butter

1. Separate the hard-cooked yolks from the whites and place in separate bowls.

2. Mash the yolks with the tines of a fork. Add mayonnaise, mustard, curry powder, and chopped shallots, and mix well. Add

more mayonnaise if needed to make a thick paste. Season with salt and pepper.

3. Mash egg whites with the tines of a fork.
4. Generously butter the bread.
5. Spread the 6 slices of white bread with the egg yolk mixture. Cover with the mashed egg white and top with whole-wheat slices.
6. Trim crusts and cut each into two finger sandwiches.

▨ Deviled Ham Sandwiches

MAKES 12 SANDWICHES

½ pound boiled ham or Virginia ham
1 teaspoon Dijon mustard
1 tablespoon mayonnaise
1 tablespoon sweet pickle relish

12 slices thinly sliced white or whole wheat bread
soft butter

1. Mince ham in container of food processor. Transfer to a bowl.
2. Blend in mustard, mayonnaise, and pickle relish. Add more mayonnaise if needed.
3. Spread bread generously with butter.
4. Cover half the slices with the ham mixture and top with remaining slices.
5. Trim crusts and cut into finger sandwiches.

▨ Fresh Mushroom Sandwiches

MAKES 24 TRIANGLES

1 pound small fresh mushrooms
1 tablespoon lemon juice
salt and freshly ground pepper
watercress butter (page 162) at room temperature

1 tablespoon finely chopped shallots
24 slices thinly sliced whole wheat bread

1. Wipe mushrooms clean with a damp towel. Leave stems a scant ½ inch long. Slice mushrooms thinly. Sprinkle with lemon juice, salt, and pepper.

2. Mix watercress butter with chopped shallots.

3. Spread one side of bread slices with watercress butter. Cover 12 of the slices with sliced mushrooms, overlapping them, and top with remaining bread slices.

4. Trim crusts and cut sandwiches into triangles. Store according to directions on page 36.

⊠ Smoked Pheasant Sandwiches with Walnuts

Each Christmas for many years I have been receiving a gift of smoked pheasants. I discovered only recently that they made wonderful sandwiches. Smoked turkey or smoked chicken breasts may be substituted if no one sends you smoked pheasants.

MAKES 48 SMALL SANDWICHES

watercress butter (page 162)
½ cup finely chopped walnuts
2 smoked pheasants or 1 pound
  smoked turkey or chicken breasts

3 tablespoons mayonnaise
24 slices very thin whole wheat bread

1. Let watercress butter soften to room temperature.

2. Toast chopped walnuts in a 350° oven for 5 to 10 minutes and set aside.

3. Remove pheasant meat from carcasses and cut into small pieces. Smoked turkey or chicken should likewise be cut into small pieces. Place in container of food processor, using the steel blade, and process with a few on-and-off turns until fairly fine. (The pheasant will shred because of the nature of the meat.)

4. Transfer to a bowl and mix in chopped walnuts and mayonnaise.

5. Butter bread slices with watercress butter. Spread 1 generous tablespoon poultry mixture over half the slices and cover with remaining slices. With a sharp knife, trim away crusts. Cut sandwiches into halves or triangles. The oblongs or triangles may also be divided in two.

6. Store according to directions on page 36.

◙ Marmalade Toast

A gussied-up version of a favorite teatime standby.

SERVES 5 OR 6

12 slices very thin white bread
orange marmalade

¼ pound (1 stick) butter, melted
confectioner's sugar

1. Trim crusts from bread and flatten slices with a rolling pin.
2. Spread slices generously with orange marmalade.
3. Starting at a corner, roll loosely into a tube with slanted ends. The marmalade will make the bread adhere to itself.
4. Brush rolls all over with melted butter and place on baking sheet. Chill in refrigerator for 1 hour.
5. Preheat broiler.
6. Broil 2 inches from heating unit until golden brown. Turn to toast the other side. Watch carefully to avoid burning.
7. Sprinkle with confectioner's sugar. Serve warm.

◙ Minced Chicken Sandwiches

These are excellent sandwiches for tea, cocktail receptions, or other occasions when the hors d'oeuvres need to be fairly substantial.

MAKES 48 SMALL SANDWICHES

4- to 5-pound chicken
3 cups chicken broth
1 large onion, peeled and cut in
  quarters
2 stalks celery, cut in halves
mayonnaise (page 161)

½ cup finely chopped celery
salt and freshly ground pepper
24 slices thinly sliced white bread
soft butter
1 teaspoon Dijon mustard

1. Wash chicken and place in a large kettle with broth, onion, and celery. Bring to a boil slowly, skimming as necessary. Reduce heat, cover pot, and simmer slowly until chicken is tender, 1 to 1¼ hours.
2. Remove chicken from broth and let cool. Strain broth, discarding vegetables. (Refrigerate or freeze broth when cooled, and reserve for your next soup-making session.)

Sandwiches, Plain and Fancy **39**

3. When chicken is cool enough to handle, trim meat from bones. Cut coarsely in pieces and place in container of food processor. Process finely with a few on-and-off turns. Do not over-process; chicken should be finely chopped enough to spread easily but not be mushy.

4. Transfer to a bowl and blend in 2 to 3 tablespoons mayonnaise — enough to bind it — and chopped celery, mixing well. Season with salt and pepper to taste.

5. Spread half the bread slices with butter, and the remaining 12 slices with mayonnaise to which 1 teaspoon of mustard has been added.

6. Spread 1 generous tablespoon of chicken mixture over the buttered slices. Cover with the mayonnaise-coated slice. With a sharp knife, trim away crusts. Cut sandwiches into halves or triangles. The oblongs or triangles may also be divided in two.

7. Arrange sandwiches on a platter or in a pan, covering each layer with dampened paper towels. They can be made well in advance and refrigerated. Remove from refrigerator at least ½ hour before serving, but keep covered until ready to serve.

▨ Cucumber Sandwiches

Light, tart, refreshing, equally popular with my carnivorous as well as my vegetarian friends.

MAKES 24 SANDWICHES

DILL BUTTER
*12 tablespoons (1½ sticks) salted
    butter*
½ cup finely chopped dill

1 large seedless cucumber
¼ cup sherry wine vinegar
1 tablespoon salt

*24 slices thin sliced white bread cut
    into 2-inch rounds*
½ cup finely chopped parsley

1. Place butter and chopped dill in container of food processor, using the steel blade. Process with a few on-and-off turns until smooth. Set aside.

2. Peel cucumber and cut into ¼-inch rounds.

3. Toss cucumber slices in a bowl with vinegar and salt, and drain immediately.

4. Spread one side of each bread round with dill butter. Place a cucumber slice between buttered sides of two bread rounds.

5. Roll the outside edge of each sandwich in chopped parsley.

6. Store according to directions on page 36.

⊠ Mixed Vegetable Tea Sandwiches

A taste treat for vegetarians — and for nonvegetarians.

MAKES 24 TEA SANDWICHES

1 medium cucumber, peeled and seeded
1 small onion, peeled
1 small carrot, scraped
1 small green bell pepper, cored and seeded
1 tablespoon unflavored gelatin

1 cup mayonnaise, preferably home-made
1 teaspoon Dijon mustard
salt and white pepper
24 slices thin white bread
soft butter

1. Finely grate cucumber and onion. Coarsely grate carrot. Finely mince green pepper. Place vegetables in a tea towel or fine mesh strainer and squeeze out juice. Reserve 3 to 4 tablespoons of juice to dissolve gelatin.

2. Sprinkle gelatin over reserved juice to soften. Heat over hot water until gelatin particles are dissolved and the liquid is clear.

3. Add gelatin to prepared vegetables. Fold in mayonnaise and mustard, and blend well. Season with salt and pepper to taste. Refrigerate overnight to give the flavors time to blend.

4. When ready to assemble, butter bread lightly. Cover 12 slices with vegetable spread and top with remaining slices. Trim away crusts with a sharp knife. Cut sandwiches in triangles or oblongs.

⊠ Rolled Watercress Sandwiches

MAKES 24 SANDWICHES

1 bunch watercress
8 ounces cream cheese at room temperature

1 tablespoon chopped chives
1 teaspoon heavy cream (optional)
24 slices thinly sliced white bread

1. Rinse watercress and pat dry. Set aside about one-third of the watercress sprigs for garnish. Finely chop the remaining leaves and stems.

2. Mash cream cheese until soft. Blend in chopped watercress and chopped chives. If mixture seems a bit thick for spreading, thin with 1 teaspoon heavy cream.

3. Trim crusts from bread. Flatten slices with a rolling pin.

4. Spread each slice with cream cheese mixture.

5. Place sprigs of watercress along the bottom edge of each slice of bread with the leaves extending beyond the edges of the bread and roll tightly. The cheese will make the bread adhere.

6. Store according to directions on page 36. Remove from refrigerator about 1 hour before serving.

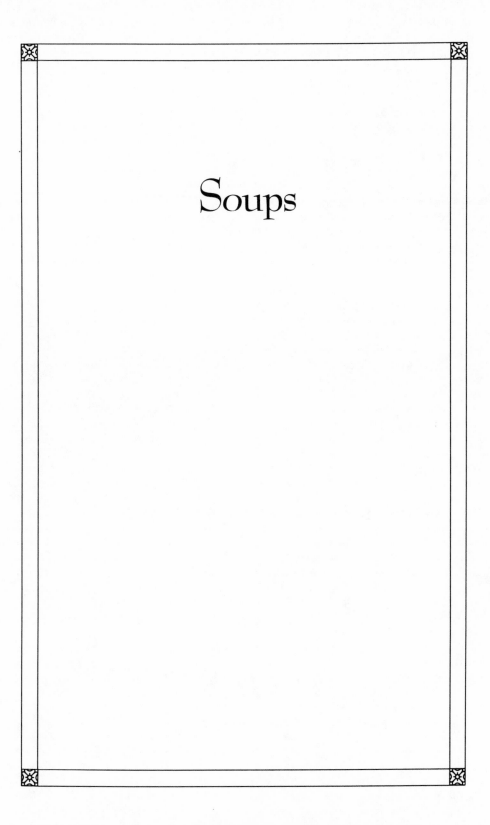

Soups

⊠ Beef Barley Soup

A hearty soup to soften the biting edge of winter and serve as the main event of lunch or supper. Accompany with a green salad and a substantial dessert.

SERVES 6 TO 8

2 ounces dried mushrooms
2 tablespoons vegetable oil
1 tablespoon finely chopped garlic
3 pounds short ribs of beef, cut into 6 or 8 pieces
2 tablespoons butter
1 pound fresh mushrooms, coarsely chopped (including stems)
1 cup chopped onions
2 cups carrots, scraped and coarsely chopped

2 cups celery with leaves, coarsely chopped
1/2 cup dried baby lima beans
1/2 cup barley, washed and drained
1/2 cup chopped fresh parsley
6 cups water
6 cups beef broth
1 bay leaf
salt and freshly ground pepper

1. Rinse dried mushrooms under cold running water. When thoroughly clean, soak in hot water for 30 minutes. Drain, reserving water, and chop coarsely. Set aside.

2. In a large soup kettle, heat oil and cook chopped garlic briefly. Do not brown.

3. Add short ribs and brown lightly.

4. In a large skillet, heat butter. Sauté fresh mushrooms, onions, and dried mushrooms until onions are limp, about 10 minutes.

5. Add to soup kettle with carrots, celery, lima beans, barley, parsley, water (include the water in which the mushrooms soaked), beef broth, and bay leaf.

6. Bring slowly to a boil, reduce heat, and simmer, partly covered, for 2 to 2½ hours. Season to taste with salt and pepper. Add additional beef broth if the soup cooks down.

7. Remove beef bones with kitchen tongs. Pick meat from bones and return to soup.

▨ Cabbage Soup *#* c̄ mustard !

A hearty, vegetable-studded soup that can serve as a main course for lunch or light supper. I recommend using the curly-headed savoy cabbage, if available. It is more flavorful and delicate than the smooth-leaved green or white variety, although it, too, will make a good soup.

SERVES 6 TO 8

10 cups chicken broth, fresh or canned
4 cups savoy (or regular) cabbage, finely shredded
2 large potatoes, peeled and diced
3 stalks celery, diced

3 carrots, scraped and diced
2 medium onions, chopped
1 leek, white part only, diced
1 parsnip, scraped and diced
2 tablespoons chopped parsley
salt and freshly ground pepper

1. Combine all ingredients in a 4-quart kettle and bring to a boil.
2. Lower heat, cover pot, and simmer gently until all vegetables are tender, about 45 minutes.
3. Taste for seasoning and correct. Serve hot.

▨ Chicken Gumbo

Okra and tomatoes grew in my mother's garden and chickens pecked around in the backyard, so this soup frequently appeared on our table as the main course. Fresh okra is generally available in the spring and summer, but the frozen will do if you can't find the fresh. I like cornbread as an accompaniment.

SERVES 6 TO 8

1 pound fresh okra
3 tablespoons flour
3 tablespoons butter
2 3-pound whole chickens
4 cups chicken broth
1 whole onion, peeled
1 carrot, scraped
1 stalk celery, cut in two
2 cups chopped onions
1 cup chopped scallions, green and white parts

1 cup chopped green peppers
1 cup chopped red peppers
2 pounds tomatoes, fresh or canned, peeled, drained, and chopped
1/2 cup chopped fresh parsley
1 teaspoon dried thyme
1 bay leaf
1 tablespoon Worcestershire sauce
salt and freshly ground pepper
4 cups steamed rice

1. Wash okra and cut or snap off stems. Slice into ½-inch slices.

2. Dredge okra slices in flour and brown lightly in butter. Set aside.

3. Rinse chickens inside and out. Trim away fat at the neck and other cavities. Place chickens in a large kettle with chicken broth, whole onion, carrot, and celery stalk. Add more water if needed to cover and cook slowly until tender, partly covered.

4. Remove chickens from kettle and let cool.

5. Skim fat from broth and discard vegetables. Return broth to kettle.

6. Skin chickens. Strip meat from the bones and cut into large pieces.

7. Add remaining vegetables, herbs, and Worcestershire sauce to chicken broth and cook until tender, 30 to 40 minutes. Add more broth if needed. Add salt and pepper to taste.

8. Add chicken for the last 15 minutes of cooking.

9. To serve, place a mound of rice in the center of each soup bowl and surround with gumbo.

◈ Corn Chowder

I like to make this soup when fresh corn is in season, although the frozen corn on the cob is acceptable. We have here two versions — one a cream style and the other a tomato vegetable chowder.

SERVES 6

8 to 10 ears of corn	1 cup onions, finely chopped
4 strips of bacon	8 cups chicken broth
1 cup celery, cut in small cubes	salt and freshly ground pepper
1 cup carrots, cut in small cubes	1½ to 2 cups cream
1 cup potatoes, peeled and cut in small cubes	chopped fresh parsley

1. Remove husks and silk from corn. With a sharp knife scraping upward, slice corn kernels into a bowl. With the back of the knife scraping downward, scrape remaining part of the kernels and the milk from the cob into the same bowl.

2. In a large soup pot, sauté bacon until crisp, leaving the rendered fat in the pot. Crumble the bacon slices and set aside.

3. To the soup pot add corn, celery, carrots, potatoes, onions, and chicken broth. Cover pot and bring slowly to a boil. Reduce heat and simmer slowly until vegetables are tender, 25 to 30 minutes.

4. Season to taste with salt and pepper.

5. Add cream and reheat, but do not boil.

6. Garnish each serving with bacon crumbles and chopped parsley.

VARIATION

Tomato Vegetable Corn Chowder: Follow the recipe for Corn Chowder, substituting for the cream a 1-pound can of plum tomatoes, undrained and chopped. Add the tomatoes with the other vegetables.

▨ Dilled Lima Bean Soup

A soup with options: serve it hot or cold, each with its own distinctive flavor.

SERVES 6

1 cup chopped onions
4 tablespoons (1/2 stick) butter
2 10-ounce packages frozen lima
   beans, unthawed
2 cups chicken broth
1/2 cup chopped fresh dill
1 cup or more buttermilk (if soup is
   to be served cold)

1 cup or more chicken broth or half-
   and-half (if soup is to be served
   hot)
salt and freshly ground pepper
2 hard-cooked egg yolks, forced
   through a strainer

1. In a large skillet, sauté onions in butter until wilted.

2. Add frozen lima beans and chicken broth, and cook until beans are soft. Separate beans with a wooden spoon as they cook to hasten the cooking.

3. Transfer to container of food processor, add dill, and process until pureed.

4. Pour into a bowl or saucepan, depending on whether you are going to serve the soup cold or hot. If cold, thin to the desired consistency with buttermilk. Season with salt and pepper. Chill in refrigerator. If hot, thin to desired consistency with chicken broth or half-and-half. Season with salt and pepper. Heat slowly over low heat.

5. Garnish each portion with sieved egg yolk.

▨ Cream of Mushroom Soup

Easily prepared and elegant enough for a formal dinner.

SERVES 6 TO 8

¹/₄ pound (1 stick) butter	*4 cups chicken broth, fresh or canned*
2 cups chopped onions	*2 cups heavy cream*
1 pound fresh mushrooms, sliced	*salt and freshly ground pepper*

1. In a large skillet, heat butter. Add onions and mushrooms, including the stems. Reserve 12 or more mushroom slices to use as soup garnish.

2. Cover skillet and cook for 15 minutes, stirring from time to time. Remove cover and cook an additional 15 minutes, or until liquid is absorbed.

3. Transfer to container of food processor and process with a few on-and-off turns until vegetables are finely chopped but not liquefied. The soup should have texture.

4. Pour chicken broth into a large saucepan, add chopped vegetables, and bring to a boil. Reduce heat and simmer for 3 or 4 minutes. Add cream and heat through, but do not boil.

5. Add salt and pepper to taste.

6. Transfer to soup bowls and garnish each portion with slices of mushroom.

▨ Pumpkin Soup

This can be made with fresh, frozen, or canned pumpkin. If canned, be sure that it is not the sweetened and spiced variety that is used for pie. A fresh pumpkin makes an exciting presentation if it is scooped out and used as a soup tureen.

SERVES 6 TO 8

1 large pumpkin (about 4 cups
pumpkin puree)
4 cups chicken broth
2 cups thinly sliced white onions

4 tablespoons (¹/₂ stick) butter
2 cups cream
salt and freshly ground pepper
sprinkling freshly grated nutmeg

1. Cut top off pumpkin and scoop out flesh, leaving a thick shell.
2. In a large, heavy saucepan, cook pumpkin in chicken broth until soft, 30 to 35 minutes.
3. In a medium skillet, sauté the onions in butter until wilted.
4. Transfer pumpkin and broth to container of food processor, add onion, and process until smooth.
5. Return to saucepan, and add the cream and salt and pepper to taste. Heat slowly, but do not boil.
6. Sprinkle each portion with freshly grated nutmeg.

▨ Watercress, Cucumber, and Avocado Soup

SERVES 6

1 bunch watercress
4 tablespoons (¹/₂ stick) butter
1 medium onion, chopped
4 medium cucumbers, peeled, seeded,
and chopped
1 cup chicken broth

2 ripe avocados
1 tablespoon lemon juice
1 tablespoon chopped parsley
1¹/₂ to 2 cups half-and-half
salt and pepper
4 red radishes, thinly sliced

1. Wash watercress and remove and discard the thickest stems. Process until finely chopped. Leave in container of food processor.
2. Heat butter in a large skillet. Add chopped onions and sauté until wilted.

3. Add chopped cucumbers and chicken broth, and cook, stirring, until cucumber is limp. Transfer to container of food processor.

4. Peel avocados, cut into chunks, and sprinkle with lemon juice. Add to container of food processor and process until smooth.

5. Pour into a bowl and thin with half-and-half to the desired consistency.

6. Season to taste with salt and pepper. Chill in refrigerator.

7. Garnish each serving portion with sliced radishes and serve cold.

▧ Winter Vegetable Soup ✳ ✳ ✳ ✳

Rutabagas and turnips give the soup a distinctive and delicious flavor.

SERVES 6 TO 8

1 cup sliced ~~small~~ white onions
4 tablespoons (½ stick) butter
4 medium rutabagas (yellow turnips),
 peeled and cubed (about 3 cups)
4 medium potatoes, peeled and cubed
3 parsnips, scraped and cubed

3 carrots, scraped and cubed
6 cups chicken broth
– 1½ to 2 cups heavy cream or half-
 and-half
~~salt and~~ freshly ground pepper

1. In a large soup pot, cook the sliced onions in butter until wilted.

2. Add rutabagas, potatoes, parsnips, carrots, and chicken broth to the soup pot. Cover and simmer slowly until vegetables are tender.

3. Transfer contents of soup pot to container of food processor and process until smooth. (You may have to do this in two batches.)

4. Return puree to soup pot. Thin with cream to desired consistency. Season with salt and pepper to taste. Reheat slowly without boiling.

Funerary Feasts

I come from a big family that, as would be statistically expected, celebrated many births and a correspondingly large number of deaths. Each occasion evoked the appropriate sentiment, ranging from jubilation to sadness, and was observed with an outpouring of feeling. Feeling and food — lots of food, particularly at funerals. I have no recollection of any final rites, but I have complete recall of dining tables laden with heaping platters of delicious things to eat that awaited the mourners when they returned from the cemetery, the bereaved women family members heavily veiled and the men wearing black armbands.

Sweet potato pies were a popular item. To this day, they fill me with the same tender nostalgia that Proust must have experienced when he savored the melting sweetness of madeleines. There would be ten or more huge sweet potato pies prepared by different friends, each distinctive in its own way, each bearing its own signature of taste and excellence. You could be sure that among other delicacies would be trays of crisp fried chicken, a noble ham, and mountains of potato salad, approved as suitable accompaniments for ham and chicken. And surely a pumpkin pie and a coconut cake or two. I am reminded of a generously proportioned woman munching a piece of sweet potato pie at my grandfather's funeral. As she filed past the coffin with her mouth full of pie, she sighed, "My, don't he look natural." The mixture of grief and a galloping appetite made an indelible impression on one small boy.

There was always a group of loving friends and neighbors who sacrificed going to the cemetery to remain in the house and prepare for the mourners when they returned after the final obsequies to what often turned into an eating spree tinged by moments of sadness.

Meats

⊠ Beef Stew

This is my extravagant no-fail stew — meltingly tender cubes of fillet of beef and vegetables in a rich dark gravy. The tender cut of beef eliminates the need for long cooking. The potatoes are sautéed until brown and crisp, and are added to the stew just before serving.

Popovers and a tossed green salad are ideal accompaniments. I like to break open the popovers and serve the stew over them, which gives us a delicious edible sponge to sop up the gravy. However, if popovers are not feasible, serve a warm, crusty loaf of thickly sliced Italian or French bread.

SERVES 8

2½ to 3 pounds fillet of beef trimmed
    of fat and cut into 1½-inch cubes
3 tablespoons Bovril*
1 cup finely chopped onions
2 cloves garlic, finely chopped
freshly ground pepper
2 bunches celery
3 carrots
3 parsnips
16 to 18 small white onions
16 to 18 small new potatoes

16 to 18 mushroom caps
5 tablespoons vegetable oil
4 tablespoons (½ stick) butter
4 to 5 cups beef broth, fresh or
    canned
bay leaf
coarse salt
½ cup all-purpose flour
2 teaspoons butter
chopped fresh parsley for garnish

1. In a large bowl, combine meat cubes with Bovril, chopped onions, garlic, and pepper. (Bovril makes additional salt unnecessary.) Coat meat well with mixture and let stand for at least 30 minutes.

2. Prepare vegetables and set aside:

Remove the tough outer stalks of celery. Trim the roots, but leave enough root to hold the hearts together. Slice off the tops and leaves, leaving the celery hearts 5 inches long. Slice the hearts vertically into quarters. Chop enough of the celery you have cut away to make 1 cup.

Scrape carrots and cut into 1-inch-thick diagonal slices.

Scrape parsnips and cut into 1-inch-thick diagonal slices.

*Bovril is concentrated beef-flavored liquid bouillon, which comes packaged in 4.2-ounce bottles. It is available in specialty food stores and in some supermarkets.

Peel white onions. White onions are easier to peel if they have been blanched in boiling water over low heat for 5 minutes. Drain and refresh under cold water. Peel the onions and cut a cross in the root end to prevent the center from popping out during cooking.

Peel potatoes and boil in salted water for 10 minutes or until slightly tender. Drain well and return to pot. Shake pot over low heat to thoroughly dry potatoes.

Wipe mushroom caps clean. Use stems for another purpose.

3. In a Dutch oven or heavy kettle, heat 3 tablespoons oil and 3 tablespoons butter until very hot. Drain meat cubes, reserving marinade, and brown meat in the hot fat. Sauté them in batches and do not crowd. When all are brown, return them to the kettle.

4. Add to the kettle chopped celery, beef broth, and bay leaf along with the reserved marinade. The liquid should just cover the meat. Cover pot and bring to a boil. Lower heat and simmer slowly for 20 minutes.

5. While stew is cooking, heat remaining 2 tablespoons oil and 1 tablespoon butter in a large skillet. Add potatoes and sauté until brown, turning them frequently. Remove from skillet with a slotted spoon and set aside.

6. In the same skillet, brown the mushrooms and sprinkle lightly with coarse salt. Add more butter if needed.

7. After the stew has cooked for 20 minutes, add carrots, parsnips, white onions, and celery hearts and continue to simmer slowly 20 minutes longer, at which time meat and vegetables should be tender.

8. In a small bowl, mix ½ cup flour, 2 teaspoons butter, and enough of the gravy to make a paste. Stir until smooth. Add to the kettle and stir over low heat until sauce is thickened and smooth.

9. Add browned potatoes and mushrooms, and heat through. Taste for seasoning and correct.

10. Transfer stew to a large tureen or bowl. Sprinkle top with chopped parsley and serve at once.

▧ Stuffed Cabbage

The flavor of the fennel seeds makes these cabbage rolls distinctive and utterly delicious. This makes about thirty rolls, but do not worry about leftovers; they freeze beautifully.

SERVES 8 TO 10

*1 to 2 large heads of savoy or regular
  cabbage*
2 pounds ground sirloin
1 cup finely chopped onions
1/2 cup finely chopped celery
1/4 cup finely chopped green pepper
1/4 cup finely chopped red pepper
*1 tablespoon fennel seeds, ground or
  crushed in a mortar and pestle*
1 cup cooked brown rice

2 eggs, lightly beaten
1 cup rye bread crumbs*
1/4 cup chopped fresh parsley
salt and freshly ground pepper
2 tablespoons butter
2 tablespoons vegetable oil
2 1/2 cups beef broth, fresh or canned
2 tablespoons soft butter
2 tablespoons flour

1. Cut a circle around the core of the cabbage to loosen leaves. Drop cabbage into a large pot of boiling salted water and remove after 3 or 4 minutes. Separate leaves and dry on paper towels. It's a good idea to keep the pot of boiling water on the stove, because sometimes as you get into the center of the cabbage it needs another immersion. (You will end up with leaves in the very center of the cabbage that are too small for stuffing. They can be chopped and cooked in a little butter and cream, providing a vegetable for another meal.)

2. Lay leaves out flat, and with a sharp paring knife or kitchen scissors cut out a small V from the root end to remove the tough vein.

3. In a mixing bowl, mix together ground meat, onions, celery, green and red peppers, fennel seeds, brown rice, and eggs, and blend well with your hands.

4. Mix in bread crumbs and chopped parsley. Season to taste with salt and pepper.

5. Place about 2 tablespoons filling — approximately the size of an egg — in the center of a cabbage leaf. Use two if they are not large. Fold in the sides and roll to make a tidy, sausage-shaped

*To make rye bread crumbs, crisp about 3 slices of rye bread (with or without crusts) on a baking sheet in a 250° oven until dried. Cut the bread into cubes and blend or process until uniformly fine.

roll. Continue until all the cabbage leaves and filling have been used.

6. Preheat oven to 350°.

7. In a large skillet, heat butter and oil. Brown cabbage rolls on both sides, turning carefully with kitchen tongs. As they are done, place them seam side down in a baking pan large enough to hold rolls snugly in a single layer.

8. Cover rolls with beef broth. Cover pan tightly with aluminum foil and bake for 1½ hours.

9. Remove pan from oven and pour off sauce into a small saucepan. Thicken sauce with a paste made of 2 tablespoons soft butter and 2 tablespoons flour. This is known as *beurre manié,* or kneaded butter (see also page 83). With your fingers, quickly knead together the flour and butter until it forms a ball. Break off small pieces, a few at a time, and stir them into the simmering sauce. Stir after each addition until each is absorbed and you reach the thickness desired.

10. Pour some of the sauce over the rolls and pass the remainder in a sauce boat.

⬚ Savory Meat Loaf

Meat loaf is a useful item in the family larder. This flavorful meat preparation is good hot or cold and for impromptu picnics. The leftovers are wonderful for household members stricken with sudden hunger pangs.

SERVES 6 TO 8

3 tablespoons vegetable oil
1 cup finely chopped onions
1 cup finely chopped celery
2 pounds ground sirloin steak
1½ cups Herb-Flavored Pepperidge
  Farm stuffing, finely ground*

2 eggs, lightly beaten
1 teaspoon powdered sage
1 teaspoon dried thyme
¼ cup chopped fresh parsley
½ cup seltzer water
salt and freshly ground pepper

*For 1½ cups of crumbs, you will need about half of an 8-ounce package of Pepperidge Farm stuffing mix. Process the stuffing mix in a food processor or blender until uniformly fine.

SAUCE

1 cup tomato sauce
2 tablespoons dark brown sugar
2 tablespoons soy sauce

1 medium onion, thinly sliced and
separated into rings

1. Preheat oven to 400°.

2. In a medium-size skillet, heat oil. Add onions and celery, and cook until softened but not brown — 7 or 8 minutes. Remove from heat and let cool.

3. In a large bowl, combine chopped beef, stuffing crumbs, eggs, sage, thyme, parsley, seltzer water, and cooked onions and celery. Mix thoroughly with your hands until all ingredients are blended and mixture is light and spongy. Add salt and pepper to taste.

4. Mound into a loaf on a lightly oiled, shallow baking pan.

5. For sauce, mix together tomato sauce, brown sugar, and soy sauce. Spread half the sauce over entire surface of meat loaf and carefully arrange onion rings over all.

6. Bake for 30 minutes. Remove from oven, cover loaf with remaining sauce, and return to oven. Reduce heat to 375° and bake 30 minutes longer.

▧ Meat and Potato Pie

A substantial supper dish for family or an informal get-together with friends.

SERVES 6 TO 8

¼ cup vegetable oil
1 cup coarsely chopped onions
1 cup coarsely chopped celery
½ cup chopped green pepper

2 pounds ground sirloin
½ cup tomato sauce
1 teaspoon ground rosemary
salt and freshly ground pepper

TOPPING

5 large potatoes, peeled and boiled
¼ cup (½ stick) melted butter
⅔ cup grated Parmesan cheese

¼ cup heavy cream
salt and freshly ground pepper
paprika

1. In a large skillet or Dutch oven, heat oil. Add onions, celery, and green pepper, mix well, and cook for 5 minutes, stirring a few times so that vegetables cook evenly.

2. Add ground beef, and continue to cook and stir until the meat loses its raw look.

3. Mix in tomato sauce and rosemary. Season to taste with salt and pepper.

4. Transfer to a lightly oiled casserole — a 9- by 13- by 2-inch rectangle or a deep 10-inch pie plate will do nicely.

5. Preheat oven to 375°.

6. Mash boiled potatoes until smooth. Add melted butter, ½ cup of the Parmesan cheese, and the heavy cream. Beat until light and fluffy. Season to taste with salt and pepper.

7. Spread potato topping over meat and smooth with a spatula. With the tines of a fork, draw diagonal lines on topping, sprinkle with remaining Parmesan cheese, and dust with paprika.

8. Bake 40 to 45 minutes, or until topping is golden brown.

▨ Pot Roast with Double-Rich Gravy

A wonderfully rich, aromatic gravy with a secret ingredient. For best results, the meat should be cooked early in the day or even the day before to ensure a completely fat-free gravy. The meat can be sliced cold and reheated in the finished gravy.

SERVES 10 TO 12

6- to 7-pound brisket (preferably first cut)
2 ounces Bovril*
1 tablespoon dark brown sugar
5 cups beef bouillon, homemade or canned
¼ cup wine vinegar
2 cups chopped onions

2 cloves garlic, crushed
2 bay leaves
freshly ground black pepper
2 tablespoons vegetable oil
5 tablespoons butter
5 tablespoons flour
salt if needed

*Bovril is the secret ingredient in this preparation. Bovril is concentrated beef-flavored liquid bouillon, which comes packaged in 4.2-ounce bottles. It is available in specialty food stores and in some supermarkets.

1. Wipe meat with a wet paper towel, and trim away some of the layer of fat that covers the top surface.

2. Mix together Bovril and brown sugar, and rub generously over all surfaces of meat.

3. In a casserole or Dutch oven with a cover, and large enough to hold the meat flat, combine the bouillon, vinegar, onions, garlic, bay leaves, and black pepper, and mix well. Place meat in marinade, cover, and refrigerate overnight. (You may also place the meat and marinade in a heavy plastic bag, tightly sealed. Put the bag on a platter in case of a leak or spillage.)

4. When ready to cook, remove meat from marinade and pat dry. Let come to room temperature.

5. Heat oil in casserole and brown meat well on all sides.

6. Pour marinade over meat. The marinade should just about cover the meat. If it doesn't, add water or more bouillon to the required depth. Cover pot and bring to a boil.

7. Reduce heat under pot and simmer very slowly for 3 hours or until meat tests tender when pierced with a fork.

8. Remove meat from pot when done and set aside. Strain liquid, discarding solids, and skim fat from surface when cooled. Ideally, the gravy should be refrigerated when cool, giving the fat time to rise to the surface and form a crust, making the skimming a simple matter.

9. Measure 5 cups of liquid for the gravy. (If you have more than that, freeze the excess and use it as a base for your next brown gravy.) Set aside.

10. In a medium-size saucepan, melt butter over medium low heat. Blend in flour, using a wire whisk. Continue to whisk and cook for 2 or 3 minutes until the flour and butter foam and bubble. Remove from heat, add the liquid all at once, and beat vigorously with wire whisk to blend smoothly. Return saucepan to moderately high heat and bring to a boil. Reduce heat and continue to whisk until sauce is thickened and smooth, 8 to 10 minutes longer. The gravy should be the consistency of heavy cream. Taste to see if it needs additional salt and pepper.

11. Slice meat against the grain in thin slices and place in a large skillet, if it needs reheating. Pour some gravy over meat and heat through, covered. Serve extra sauce in a sauceboat.

⊠ Stuffed Fillet of Beef with Shallot Sauce

A fine dish for a special occasion. The meat is rolled around a spinach filling, which makes the cut slices most attractive with swirls of green contrasting with the brown and rosy meat. The beef is cooked in two stages; the final cooking is brief and need not be started until all the dinner guests have arrived, thereby saving you the trauma of serving overdone beef.

SERVES 8

5- to 6-pound fillet of beef
1 large garlic clove, crushed

soft butter
salt and freshly ground pepper

FILLING

1½ pounds fresh spinach or 2
  10-ounce packages frozen
½ cup chicken broth
1 tablespoon oil
1 tablespoon butter

1 large onion, finely chopped
1 egg, lightly beaten
½ cup fine bread crumbs
salt and freshly ground pepper

SHALLOT SAUCE

¼ cup chopped shallots
2 tablespoons butter
2 tablespoons cognac

1 cup heavy cream
2 tablespoons Dijon mustard
salt and pepper

1. Trim excess fat and membrane from fillet. Place beef on flat surface. With the knife held parallel to the table top, cut fillet in two from top to tail end, but do not cut all the way through. (Your butcher can do this for you.) Spread meat out and place between two sheets of wax paper. Pound very lightly to flatten a bit, in preparation for rolling. Handle gently.

2. For the filling, wash spinach in several waters to remove sand. Cut off coarse stems. Cook spinach in chicken broth until just wilted. If using frozen spinach, cook in broth until thawed. Drain through a strainer, pressing out moisture with the back of a spoon.

3. Chop spinach when cool enough to handle.

4. In a small skillet, heat oil and butter. Add onion and sauté until limp.

5. Add onion, egg, and bread crumbs to chopped spinach, and mix well. Add salt and pepper to taste.

6. Spread spinach mixture evenly over the entire surface of meat, leaving a narrow strip uncovered along the long outside edge so there will be some lap to seal the roll. Roll meat like a jelly roll. Tie at intervals with butcher's twine. Trim ragged edges along the two short ends to make the roll tidy.

7. Heat broiler to highest heat.

8. Rub meat roll with garlic clove and spread softened butter generously over all surfaces. Sprinkle with salt and pepper.

9. Transfer meat to a shallow baking pan and place pan 3 inches below source of heat. Broil for 10 minutes on each side, turning meat with kitchen tongs. Remove from broiler and set aside. This step may be done 1 hour or longer before serving time.

10. Preheat oven to 375° 40 minutes before serving time. Place meat in oven and bake for about 20 minutes, or until meat reaches the desired degree of doneness. When cooked as you like it, remove from oven, tent loosely with aluminum foil, and allow to rest for 10 to 15 minutes to give its juices time to settle. It will also continue to cook with its own stored-up heat.

11. For the shallot sauce, sauté chopped shallots in butter until limp. Add cognac and stir to dissolve any brown particles clinging to the bottom and sides of the pan.

12. Mix together heavy cream and mustard in a small saucepan. Cook until slightly thickened, but do not boil.

13. Add shallot mixture to cream and warm through. Taste for seasoning and add salt and pepper as needed.

14. Remove strings from meat roll. Cut meat into slices about ³⁄₈ inch thick. Arrange on warmed platter garnished with watercress. Serve sauce separately in a sauceboat.

▨ Hearty Spaghetti Meat Sauce

A delicious meat sauce that will transform a bowl of spaghetti into a substantial main course. It serves equally well as a sauce for lasagna. It can be frozen in small containers and be on the ready for unexpected guests.

MAKES 2 QUARTS OF SAUCE

*6 medium-size Italian sweet sausages
(about 1 pound)*
½ cup good-quality olive oil
1 cup chopped onions
*1 bunch chopped scallions (green and
white parts)*
2 carrots, scraped and finely chopped
½ cup finely chopped celery
3 cloves garlic, finely chopped
2 pounds chopped sirloin
*28-ounce can Italian peeled tomatoes,
undrained and crushed*

6-ounce can tomato paste
½ cup chopped flat parsley
1 bay leaf
1 tablespoon dried oregano
*1 tablespoon dried basil, or 3 table-
spoons chopped fresh basil*
1 tablespoon sugar
½ cup dry red wine
salt and freshly ground pepper

1. Remove sausage meat from casing and cut into ¼-inch rounds.

2. In a heavy kettle or Dutch oven, heat 1 or 2 tablespoons oil — just enough to lightly film the bottom of the pan — and brown sausage meat well, turning it to cook on all sides.

3. Add remaining oil and sauté onions, scallions, carrots, celery, and garlic until limp and transparent, but do not brown.

4. Add chopped meat, and cook and stir until it loses its raw look.

5. Stir in crushed tomatoes and liquid, tomato paste, parsley, bay leaf, oregano, basil, sugar, and wine. Add salt and pepper as needed.

6. Bring to a boil, lower heat, and simmer slowly for 2 hours, uncovered. Stir from time to time to make sure the sauce is not scorching. Taste and correct seasoning.

⊠ Roast Leg of Lamb with Rosemary

SERVES 6 TO 8

5- to 6-pound leg of lamb
2 tablespoons olive oil
1 teaspoon dried rosemary
*2 cloves garlic, crushed and finely
minced*
1 cup chopped onions

1 cup chopped carrots
salt and freshly ground pepper
2 tablespoons flour
1 cup water
1 tablespoon soft butter

1. Trim excess fat from leg and peel off outer membrane (fell). Rub meat with olive oil, rosemary, and garlic. Let meat rest at room temperature for 1 or 2 hours.

2. Preheat oven to 400°.

3. Spread chopped onions and carrots over bottom of roasting pan.

4. Place meat over bed of vegetables and roast for 45 minutes. Reduce heat to 350°, and continue roasting for an additional 30 minutes for rare to medium meat, 45 to 50 minutes for medium to well-done.

5. Sprinkle meat with salt and pepper, and remove from oven. Let meat rest in a warm place for 15 minutes to let juices settle.

6. Strain pan drippings and return to baking pan. Add flour and blend well. Add water and stir with wire whisk until well blended. Swirl in soft butter. Taste for seasoning and correct.

7. Slice meat thinly, transfer to warmed serving platter, and serve sauce separately.

▨ Marinated Leg of Lamb

The process of marinating meats and poultry has a lot to recommend it: besides adding flavor and sparkle, it helps to tenderize. Try to allow 24 hours or more for marinating. It will do the food nothing but good.

SERVES 6 TO 8

MARINADE
1/2 cup dry red wine
1/2 cup Armagnac
2 cloves garlic, cut into slivers

1/2 cup finely chopped onion
2 tablespoons dried crushed rosemary
salt and freshly ground pepper

5- to 6-pound leg of lamb
1/4 cup olive oil
1 tablespoon coarse salt

1. Blend marinade ingredients well.

2. Trim excess fat from lamb and remove fell, the parchmentlike membrane that covers it. With a sharp-pointed knife,

make small slits in meat and insert slivers of garlic from marinade.

3. Pour marinade into a heavy plastic bag. Add lamb and secure the bag tightly. Place it on a platter or pan in case the bag springs a leak. Refrigerate overnight, turning the bag a few times.

4. Remove lamb from the refrigerator several hours before roasting to give it time to come to room temperature.

5. Preheat oven to 325°.

6. Remove meat from marinade and pat dry with paper towels. Reserve the marinade for basting. Rub lamb with olive oil and coarse salt.

7. Transfer lamb to a roasting pan and roast for 1½ hours for rare, 2 hours for medium, and 2½ hours for well done. Brush with marinade every 20 minutes.

8. When done, remove lamb from oven and let rest on a warm platter for 15 minutes before carving.

☒ Bourbon Baked Ham

A baked ham does yeoman's service for a large dinner party, a buffet, a cocktail party, or a picnic, with the added reward after the meat is eaten of a flavorful bone for some delicious pea or lentil soup.

SERVES 12 TO 15

12- to 16-pound cooked smoked whole ham with the bone
whole cloves (optional)
2 cups unsweetened pineapple juice
1 cup light brown sugar

1 cup dark brown sugar
1 cup French's prepared mustard
1 cup bourbon
1 teaspoon ground cloves

1. Preheat oven to 350°.

2. Wash and dry ham. Score the fat in diamond shapes and place a whole clove in the center of each diamond-shaped space.

3. Place in large roasting pan. Pour pineapple juice over and bake for 1 hour.

4. Remove ham from oven and pour off half of the liquid.

5. Mix the remaining ingredients.

6. Spoon half over ham and continue roasting. Baste every 15

minutes with remainder until nicely glazed, about 1½ hours additional.

7. Remove and cool completely. You can refrigerate at this point or serve. If refrigerated, remove at least 1 hour before serving and keep at room temperature.

▨ Aunt Rosie's Oven-barbecued Spareribs

Aunt Rosie was greatly admired for her oven-barbecued spareribs, reproduced below exactly as she made them. They may be served hot or cold.

SERVES 6 TO 8

2 slabs of lean spareribs, about 4 pounds each

salt and freshly ground pepper

BARBECUE SAUCE
¼ pound (1 stick) butter
2 teaspoons finely minced garlic
2 cups finely chopped onions
2 cups chili sauce
¼ cup soy sauce
1½ tablespoons chili powder or to taste

¼ teaspoon Tabasco sauce or more, to taste
¼ cup sherry wine vinegar or red wine vinegar
3 tablespoons dark brown sugar

1. Preheat oven to 400°.
2. Sprinkle spareribs lightly with salt and pepper. Arrange slabs in each of two large baking dishes. Bake 1 hour in oven. Turn ribs and bake 10 minutes longer. Pour off fat.
3. While meat is baking, heat butter in a large saucepan and add garlic and onions. Cook, stirring, until onions are limp. Add chili sauce, soy sauce, chili powder, Tabasco sauce, vinegar, and sugar. Bring to a boil, reduce heat, and simmer about 5 minutes.
4. Brush each slab of ribs on the underside with sauce and return to oven, brushed side up. Bake 30 minutes, brushing on the same side with sauce.
5. Turn the ribs. Brush generously with all the remaining sauce. Return to the oven and bake 30 minutes.
6. Cut the spareribs into individual rib servings.

⊠ Crown Roast of Pork Filled with Brussels Sprouts and Chestnuts

SERVES 8

crown roast of pork, about 16 chops
coarse salt and freshly ground pepper
1 large clove garlic, finely minced
1 cup Kahlúa
4 tablespoons (½ stick) butter

½ cup beef broth
2 tablespoons arrowroot
2 cups half-and-half
brussels sprouts and chestnuts
   (page 122)

1. Preheat oven to 325°.
2. Rub crown roast with salt, pepper, and garlic. Wrap tips of rib bones with aluminum foil to prevent charring.
3. In a small saucepan, combine Kahlúa, butter, and beef broth, and heat until butter is melted.
4. Place roast on a rack in a shallow baking pan and roast for 20 minutes to the pound. Baste often with Kahlúa mixture.
5. When roast is done, remove from pan and keep warm.
6. Dissolve arrowroot in half-and-half and add to the pan drippings. Stir over moderate heat just until smooth and creamy. Taste for seasonings and correct.
7. Place cooked brussels sprouts and chestnuts in the center of the crown roast. Decorate rib bones with paper frills. Pass sauce separately in sauceboat.

⊠ Breaded Veal Scallops

SERVES 4

8 thin slices veal, about 1½ pounds
⅓ cup whole wheat flour
⅓ cup all-purpose flour
salt and freshly ground pepper
1 egg, beaten
½ cup wheat germ (unsweetened)

¼ cup (½ stick) butter
¼ cup vegetable oil
3 tablespoons cognac
1 cup heavy cream or half-and-half
chopped fresh parsley

1. Place veal slices between two sheets of wax paper and pound with a flat mallet to make thinner.
2. Combine whole wheat flour, all-purpose flour, salt, and pepper. Dredge veal slices in flour mixture, shaking off excess.

3. Dip meat in beaten egg and then into wheat germ. Place on a sheet of wax paper and let rest at room temperature for 1 hour or longer.

4. In a large heavy skillet, heat butter and oil until bubbly.

5. Add meat slices in batches and cook without crowding, 3 to 4 minutes on each side, until golden brown. Set aside as they are done and keep warm.

6. Deglaze the pan with cognac, scraping with a wooden spoon to pick up all the browned particles on the bottom of the pan. Add cream or half-and-half (cream will give a thicker sauce) and stir over low heat until sauce thickens.

7. Transfer meat to a warmed platter and ladle sauce over. Sprinkle with chopped parsley.

▨ Veal Scallops with Tarragon

SERVES 4

8 thin slices veal, about 1½ pounds
salt and freshly ground pepper
3 tablespoons butter
3 tablespoons oil
¼ cup vodka

¼ cup brandy
2 tablespoons chopped fresh tarragon
  or 1 teaspoon dried tarragon
1 cup heavy cream or half-and-half

1. Place veal scallops between two sheets of wax paper and pound with a flat mallet to make thinner. Remove paper and sprinkle meat lightly with salt and pepper.

2. In a large heavy skillet, heat butter and oil until bubbly. Sauté scallops until golden brown on each side, 2 to 3 minutes on a side. Sauté only as many as will fit on the bottom of the pan without crowding. Set the cooked slices aside on a heated platter until all are done.

3. Deglaze the pan with vodka and brandy, scraping up all the browned particles on the bottom of the pan with a wooden spoon.

4. Add tarragon and cream to the pan and cook over low heat until sauce is slightly thickened. Taste and correct seasoning.

5. Transfer veal scallops to a heated platter and cover with some of the sauce. Serve the remainder in a sauceboat.

⊠ Veal Chops with Glazed Apples

SERVES 4

4 loin veal chops, about 1/2 pound each
salt and freshly ground pepper
2 tablespoons flour
5 tablespoons butter
3 tablespoons oil
1 cup apple cider
1 cup heavy cream
1/2 cup beef stock, fresh or canned
1 tablespoon Worcestershire sauce
3 Granny Smith apples
2 tablespoons granulated sugar

1. Trim away most of the fat from each chop. Season chops with salt and pepper and dredge lightly in flour, shaking off the excess.

2. Heat 3 tablespoons butter and the oil in a large heavy skillet, big enough to hold chops in one layer without crowding. When the fat bubbles, add chops and cook over moderate heat about 8 or 9 minutes. Turn chops and continue cooking the other side about 15 minutes. Remove from skillet and keep warm.

3. Deglaze the skillet with 1/2 cup cider, scraping with a wooden spoon to pick up all the browned particles on the bottom of the pan. Cook to reduce by half. Add cream, and cook and stir until reduced and thickened. Add beef stock and Worcestershire sauce, and blend well. Swirl in remaining butter.

4. While the chops are cooking, peel and core apples and cut into quarters. Preheat oven to 450°.

5. Place apple quarters on a greased cookie sheet. Sprinkle with sugar and the remaining 1/2 cup of apple cider. Bake until the apples are glazed, about 10 minutes.

6. To serve, arrange chops on a platter, pour sauce over, and garnish with the apples.

▨ Veal Stew

SERVES 6 TO 8

1 ounce dried mushrooms
2¹/₂ cups beef stock, fresh or canned
3 pounds lean veal, cut into 2-inch
cubes
salt and freshly ground pepper
4 tablespoons vegetable oil
1 teaspoon finely minced garlic
2 tablespoons tomato paste

2 tablespoons flour
3 carrots, scraped and cut into diago-
nal slices 1¹/₂ inches thick
12 to 16 small white onions,
blanched and peeled
1 cup crème fraîche or sour cream
1 tablespoon chopped fresh dill or
1 teaspoon dried

1. Rinse the mushrooms under cold running water to remove traces of sand. Drain.

2. In medium-size saucepan, bring beef stock to a boil. Remove from heat, add dried mushrooms, and allow to soak in the hot stock for 30 minutes.

3. Trim fat from veal cubes, sprinkle lightly with salt and pepper, and brown in heated oil in a large skillet. Do not crowd meat cubes in the skillet or they will steam instead of browning properly. Cook a small amount at a time and set aside as they are browned.

4. Drain soaked mushrooms, press out liquid, and set aside. Reserve stock and strain through fine dampened cheesecloth.

5. Chop mushrooms and sauté in the skillet in which you browned the meat. Add garlic, and more oil if needed. Cook until mushrooms are soft, 5 to 7 minutes.

6. Stir in the tomato paste. Stir in flour and stir until smooth. Add strained stock, sliced carrots, and blanched and peeled white onions. Return meat to skillet. Bring to a boil, reduce heat, cover, and simmer slowly until meat is tender, about 1¹/₂ hours.

7. Remove from heat; add *crème fraîche* or sour cream, and dill. Blend well. Heat gently, but do not boil. Taste for seasoning and correct.

8. Serve over buttered noodles sprinkled with poppy seeds.

⊠ Roast Fillet of Veal

An impressive main course for a gala occasion.

SERVES 8

4-pound fillet of veal
3 tablespoons butter
2 tablespoons olive oil
1 teaspoon dried rosemary
3 tablespoons Bovril*
3 garlic cloves, peeled

2 tablespoons cognac
2 tablespoons Dijon mustard
1 cup heavy cream or half-and-half
salt and pepper
minced fresh parsley

1. Wipe fillet with damp paper towel and place in a shallow baking pan.

2. Make a paste of butter, olive oil, rosemary, and Bovril, and rub mixture over fillet, coating generously. Let meat sit at room temperature for 1 to 2 hours before roasting.

3. Preheat oven to 450°.

4. Add garlic cloves to baking pan and place in preheated oven. For added convenience and an excellent result, roast meat in two stages: Well in advance of serving time, roast for 30 minutes, remove from oven, and let rest. Then return meat to a 450° oven and roast for 35 to 40 minutes before serving.

5. Remove meat from pan, tent lightly with aluminum foil, and keep warm.

6. Place baking pan on top of the stove and deglaze with cognac, loosening all the brown particles on the bottom of the pan. Add mustard and cream or half-and-half, and blend well. Season to taste with salt and pepper.

7. Slice meat and arrange on platter. Cover with sauce and sprinkle with chopped parsley.

VARIATION

Roast Fillet of Veal with Apple Rings and Onions: Follow directions for roast veal, substituting calvados (apple brandy) for the cognac.

4 Granny Smith apples
2 tablespoons granulated sugar

7 tablespoons soft butter
16 to 20 small white onions

*Bovril is a beef-flavored, concentrated liquid bouillon, available in specialty food stores and some supermarkets.

1. Peel and core apples. Slice into ½-inch rings. Sprinkle with sugar and dot with 3 tablespoons soft butter. Bake in 400° oven for about 15 minutes, until glazed. The apple rings may also be sprinkled with sugar and sautéed in butter in a skillet on top of the stove.

2. Blanch onions in boiling water for 3 or 4 minutes. Drain well and slip off the skins.

3. Heat remaining 4 tablespoons butter in a skillet, add onions, and sauté until softened and golden. Shake pan frequently so that onions will cook on all sides.

4. To serve, surround sliced meat with apple rings and onions. Serve sauce separately.

▨ Venison Stew with Sweet Potatoes and Prunes

My father's annual hunting trip around Thanksgiving time furnished the Hovis family with a generous supply of venison. He butchered the meat himself, and we had lots of stews, roasts, and even steaks that could be barbecued if the animal happened to be a buck. I have taken liberties with my mother's recipe and used a wine marinade in place of the milk she customarily used as a soak for the meat. I think she will approve of the vegetables and prunes in this version of her venison stew. It's a lovely dish for a festive occasion at holiday time.

Buttered cooked noodles sprinkled with poppy seeds and chopped parsley, a green salad, hot crusty French bread, and a good dry red wine such as Nouveau Beaujolais are fine accompaniments.

SERVES 10 TO 12

MARINADE
1 cup dry red wine
½ cup good-quality virgin olive oil
2 tablespoons lemon juice
½ cup malt vinegar
1 cup finely chopped shallots

2 tablespoons dark brown sugar
2 tablespoons Bovril*
1 tablespoon Worcestershire sauce
4 juniper berries
2 bay leaves, crumbled

*Bovril is a beef-flavored, concentrated liquid bouillon, available in specialty food stores and some supermarkets.

5 pounds venison fillets cut into 1½-inch cubes
oil for browning meat
6 cups beef broth, fresh or canned
½ cup plus 1 tablespoon all-purpose flour

2 pounds small sweet potatoes, peeled and cut into 1½-inch-thick rounds
24 small white onions, peeled
1½ pounds large pitted prunes
salt and pepper, if needed

1. In a large nonaluminum bowl — earthenware, glass, or stainless steel — combine all marinade ingredients. Add meat cubes and mix well, making sure that all are well coated. Cover bowl and refrigerate overnight.

2. When ready to cook, drain meat well, reserving the marinade. Dry meat thoroughly with paper towels.

3. Film the bottom of a large Dutch oven or heavy casserole with vegetable oil and heat over moderate heat. Brown meat cubes well on all sides. Brown only as many at a time as will fit in one layer without touching, or they will steam instead of brown. Return to casserole when all are done.

4. Combine reserved marinade and beef broth, and pour over meat. Cover pot and cook slowly for 2 hours. If you wish, this can be done well in advance of the final baking in the oven.

5. Preheat oven to 375°.

6. In a small bowl, combine flour and as much gravy as you need to dissolve the flour. Stir until smooth.

7. Skim fat from the surface of stew and add flour thickener. Stir over moderate heat until gravy is thickened and smooth.

8. Add to the stew pot the sweet potato slices, white onions, and prunes. Mix through, cover pot, and bake in preheated oven for 1 hour. Do not stir the stew while it is in the oven. Taste for seasoning and add salt and pepper, if needed.

Miss D. and My Skillet Meals

My repertoire of meals made in an electric skillet had its beginning when I first came to New York in the early 1950s, determined to find my place on the Broadway stage. I lived in a furnished room on the top floor of a narrow little house on Charles Street in Greenwich Village. To make up for the room's modest 9- by 12-foot size, there was a skylight that lent the place considerable cachet and compensated, in part, for the inconvenience of running water that was three flights below. Need I add that my funds were limited and my earnings practically nonexistent?

The room had some style, I thought. The walls were white except for one that was painted a rich, vibrant terra-cotta. My good friend Bill Smith donated draperies. They were made of drapery lining material since none of us could afford proper drapery fabric, but they were effective. One wall was covered with a display of head shots of my friends who were also aspiring and mostly unemployed actors. The bed, extravagantly covered with a variety of throw pillows cadged from heaven knows where, doubled as a couch by day. A tall vase of rhododendron leaves filled a fireplace that didn't work and probably never had. The top of every piece of furniture was covered with an adhesive-backed marbled paper to hide the peeling and cracked surfaces underneath.

Concealed by a screen, a small refrigerator salvaged from the street stood in a corner near the window. It had obviously been discarded by some captain of industry who could afford to chuck out a refrigerator that worked, even one that was slightly the worse for wear. Since there were no facilities and cooking was expressly forbidden in what I euphemistically called "my apartment," I positioned a hot plate and an electric skillet on top of the refrigerator. The window, when open, provided a perfect exhaust. I could cook away, secure in knowing that there was little danger of cooking odors to expose my lawbreaking. My room soon became the eating and meeting place for lots of my·actor friends who were between engagements, another euphemism for being out of work. Often there would be ten or twelve friends for supper. Portions were small, of necessity, but no one left hungry.

With nothing that even vaguely resembled an oven, it was impossible to bake, but I found a marvelous little home bakery on West Fourth Street that bore the name of its owner, Miss Douglas.

Her baking reminded me of Granny Dameron's. Miss Douglas was a slender, small-boned woman with bright red hair who could have come out of one of the Moulin Rouge paintings by Toulouse-Lautrec. She was distinctive and different and could easily have qualified for top billing on anybody's list of "The Most Unforgettable Character I Have Ever Known." A lady of wit and intellect and an avid reader, she had a broad knowledge of antiques, art, literature, and music, and she introduced me to the works of e. e. cummings, Chekhov, and the classical Greek dramatists.

My skillet parties always ended with a dessert from Miss D.'s. Her double fudge brownies were a popular item. As she wrapped them while we chatted about Village happenings, she would say, "Is No-Nuts coming for dinner tonight?" No-Nuts was her name for a frequent guest who was allergic to nuts. If he was expected, she would produce some brownies without nuts that she had stashed away. In the summer she made delicious peach shortcakes. They were one of my favorites, and so she named me "Peach." She also made wonderful coconut cake, chocolate fudge cake, sweet potato pie, and a melt-in-the-mouth almond coffee ring, among other fine creations.

As we talked, she would prepare the bill. Her bills were a thing of wonder. If the number nine appealed to her on a particular day, everything would cost from nine to ninety-nine cents. But over one dollar, all prices were rounded off. A cake might cost one dollar, or two dollars, but never, never, a dollar and a half. I suppose it made the arithmetic simpler. I should add that when my funds were low, which was most of the time, Miss D. would give me a discount.

Saturday was Baked Beans and Brown Bread day at Miss D.'s — a special event for which customers lined up early. A sign announcing it was taped to the window. By noon the sign was reversed and it now read, "No more Beans and Bread today. Come early next Saturday."

Miss D.'s staff consisted of two women — Naome and Dorothy. In all the years during which I visited Miss Douglas's shop, I never saw either of them, but I know they were there, working back of the louvered door that separated the kitchen from the front of the store, where Miss Douglas was in charge.

"Na-OME." Miss Douglas accented and lengthened the last syllable. "Na-OME, how are those pies?"

"They're beginning to get tanned, Miss Douglas," replied Naome.

"Don't let them look like they've been to Jamaica," cautioned Miss Douglas.

A string of "Okays" and "Yes, ma'ams" came from Naome and Dorothy, who understood that Miss Douglas was warning them not to let the pies get too brown.

Miss Douglas closed her shop in the mid-1960s. She died shortly after, deeply missed and mourned by all who knew her.

Skillet Meals

About Iron Skillets

Cooks can be as sentimental about their iron skillets as doting parents over a lock of hair saved from their first-born. And with good reason — an iron skillet that has been well cared for can be a most rewarding piece of kitchen equipment. Anyone who has ever used one is familiar with its good qualities: it absorbs heat slowly and evenly and retains it; it is heavy and consequently food will not scorch or burn quickly. The iron skillet's slow, steady heat makes it excellent for pan-broiling and baking, and it has the added advantage of being able to go into the oven.

The disadvantages are that it rusts and stains and can become pitted on exposure to air and dampness. However, all of these minor catastrophes can be avoided with proper care. You can prevent rust by washing and oiling after using it and then drying it over a stove burner. I once gave as a Christmas present an iron skillet that I had been using for five years. I was reluctant to give it up, but I couldn't refuse the request of a friend who was sentimental about all the good dishes that had been cooked in it.

▨ Poached Tabasco Eggs

This was a popular Sunday brunch dish that is still requested by friends.

SERVES 6

1/2 pound thin-sliced bacon
2 cups heavy cream
1 tablespoon Tabasco sauce

12 fresh eggs, chilled
chopped fresh parsley
hot buttered toast, cut into triangles

1. Cook bacon until crisp and drain on absorbent paper. Crumble and set aside.
2. Butter a skillet, electric or stove-top. Combine cream and Tabasco sauce, and bring to a boil. Reduce to a gentle simmer.
3. Carefully break eggs into the hot cream. Don't cook too many at a time, and distribute them in the liquid so that they don't impinge on each other. Spoon simmering cream over the eggs for 3 or 4 minutes, until whites become opaque and yolks feel just resistant to the touch.

4. Remove eggs with a slotted spoon or skimmer and keep warm on a large platter until all are done. Dribble the hot cream over the eggs and sprinkle with crumbled bacon and chopped parsley.

5. Arrange a border of buttered toast triangles around the eggs.

⊠ Skillet Meat Loaves

Individual meat loaves cooked in a skillet, electric or stove-top. Unlike the usual meat loaf, which is oven-baked, these can be described as being potted or braised.

SERVES 6

6 tablespoons vegetable oil
1/2 cup finely chopped onions
1/4 cup finely chopped green peppers
1/4 cup finely chopped red peppers
1/4 cup finely chopped celery
2 pounds ground sirloin
1/2 cup fine bread crumbs
1 teaspoon thyme

1 tablespoon chopped fresh parsley
2 eggs, lightly beaten
1/4 cup seltzer water
salt and freshly ground pepper
3 tablespoons butter
1/2 cup beef broth, fresh or canned
1 to 2 tablespoons Dijon mustard
3 tablespoons heavy cream

1. Heat 3 tablespoons oil in the skillet and sauté onions, peppers, and celery until wilted. Remove from skillet and cool. Do not clean skillet.

2. Place meat in a large bowl. Add cooled, cooked vegetables, bread crumbs, thyme, parsley, eggs, and seltzer water. Mix well, preferably using your hands. Season to taste with salt and pepper.

3. Divide meat into 6 equal portions. Mold each into an oval-shaped loaf.

4. Heat remaining 3 tablespoons oil and the butter in skillet, and brown meat loaves on all sides.

5. Pour beef broth over meat loaves, cover skillet, and cook for 45 minutes.

6. Remove meat loaves from skillet and keep warm. Increase heat and boil sauce to reduce. Lower heat and stir in 1 to 2 tablespoons Dijon mustard and heavy cream. Mix well. Return meat loaves to skillet and baste each with sauce. Serve from skillet.

⊠ Stuffed Peppers

During my unemployed-actor period, I used to split the peppers in half, horizontally, thereby doubling the quantity, at least visually. It's still a good idea for a buffet when there are a number of other dishes and a whole stuffed pepper would be excessive.

SERVES 6

6 red and green bell peppers
4 tablespoons vegetable oil
1/2 cup finely chopped shallots
1/2 cup finely chopped celery
1 pound ground sirloin
1/2 cup cooked rice
1/4 cup dry bread crumbs
2 eggs, lightly beaten

2 tablespoons chopped fresh parsley
salt and freshly ground pepper
2 cups peeled fresh or canned tomatoes, crushed
1/2 cup beef broth, fresh or canned
1/4 cup dry red wine
beurre manié,* to thicken sauce

1. Wash peppers, cut off slice from the stem end, and remove seeds and heavy membranes. Drain well and dry on paper towels. Set aside.

2. Heat oil in the skillet and sauté shallots and celery until tender. Cool. Do not clean skillet.

3. Place meat in a bowl. Add cooled vegetables, rice, bread crumbs, eggs, and parsley, and mix well with your hands. Add salt and pepper to taste.

4. Fill pepper shells with meat mixture. Transfer to skillet.

5. In a bowl, combine crushed tomatoes, beef broth, and wine. Blend well, and taste for seasoning and correct. Pour over and around peppers.

6. Cover skillet and cook over low heat for 50 minutes to 1 hour, or until peppers are tender. If sauce is too thin, thicken it with a *beurre manié.*

7. Serve from skillet.

*Beurre manié, or kneaded butter, can be a kitchen lifesaver, rescuing sauces that have failed to thicken properly. Knead together equal parts of butter and flour (such as 4 tablespoons of each) until they form a thick paste that can be shaped into a ball. Break off small pieces of the paste, a few at a time, and stir them into the simmering liquid. The thickening takes place very quickly. Stop the cooking as soon as the sauce is thick and smooth. *Beurre manié* can be stored in a covered jar in the refrigerator for two or three weeks with no damage.

▨ Skillet Pork Chops

A one-dish meal that looks good and tastes good.

12 thinly sliced pork chops
¼ cup soy sauce
3 tablespoons olive oil
3 tablespoons vegetable oil
freshly ground pepper

1 medium onion, thinly sliced
3 medium potatoes, peeled and
   quartered
3 carrots, scraped and thinly sliced
1½ cups beef broth

1. Wipe chops with damp paper towel and pat dry.
2. Marinate chops in soy sauce for 30 minutes. Make sure that each chop is coated with sauce.
3. Heat olive oil and vegetable oil in skillet. Brown chops on both sides, in batches. Set them aside as they are browned.
4. Return browned chops to skillet and arrange carefully, overlapping them. Sprinkle with pepper.
5. Add sliced onion and brown quickly.
6. Add potatoes, carrots, and beef broth. Cover and cook until vegetables are tender, about 15 minutes.
7. Remove cover and cook at high heat for a few minutes to reduce gravy.
8. Serve in skillet.

Poultry
and
Dressings

Poultry

Chicken was always a favorite in my mother's household, as it still is in mine. We raised our own birds, and I recall what a treat it was for me to feed them as a youngster. I loved sprinkling the food about and watching the little creatures, heads bobbing, scratching around to devour every single grain. And for some reason I can't explain, I took enormous pleasure in hearing the hens' loud cackling when they announced they were fulfilling their mission in life by producing an egg. I guess they were pleased with themselves and I was pleased for them.

Among the profusion of delectables on my mother's Sunday dinner table would be heaping platters of chicken — crisp, golden-brown fried chicken. We could be as sure of this as that one of the guests would be a preacher, either our own or one visiting from a neighboring town. My parents entertained an unending succession of preacher guests on Sundays, all of whom seemed to share a passion for the Hovis fried chicken — which was why we named it "Gospel Bird."

Aside from the chords of nostalgia that thoughts of my mother's Sunday dinners evoke, there's a great deal to be said about chicken these days. Besides its fine nutritional record in these calorie-cholesterol-conscious days, chicken is one of the few foods whose cost has not zoomed into the stratosphere. And it lends itself to such a variety of preparations that it can provide a different eating experience every time it is served. Chicken can be broiled, baked, fried, stewed, or barbecued; it can be cooked in a brown sauce, a white sauce, a red sauce, or no sauce; and it combines wonderfully with a variety of vegetables or fruits. Its possibilities are infinite.

▨ Crisp Baked Breast of Chicken

SERVES 4 TO 6

3 whole boneless chicken breasts
2 whole eggs
3 tablespoons water
2 cups crushed potato chips

1 tablespoon dried oregano
freshly ground pepper
4 tablespoons (1/2 stick) butter, melted

1. Preheat oven to 375°. Butter a flat baking sheet.

2. Divide chicken breasts in half. Trim tabs of fat. Rinse breasts and pat dry. (The breasts may be cooked with or without the skin, as you prefer.)

3. Beat eggs with water in a shallow bowl.

4. Place potato chips between 2 sheets of wax paper or in a plastic bag. With a rolling pin, crush potato chips into coarse crumbs.

5. Combine crumbs with oregano and pepper. (The potato chips will provide sufficient salt.) Spread a small amount of crumbs at a time on a sheet of wax paper.

6. Dip chicken breasts in beaten egg, letting excess drip back in the bowl. Roll in crumbs, patting them down with your fingers. Add more dry crumbs as needed.

7. Place chicken breasts on baking sheet. Dribble melted butter over breasts and bake for 50 to 60 minutes, until nicely browned and crisp.

⊠ Chicken Breasts in Orange-Cognac Sauce

A quick preparation that looks like an elaborate, time-consuming one. Serve the glazed chicken breasts on a mound of fluffy rice with snow peas or broccoli flowerets and steamed whole baby carrots for color contrast.

SERVES 4 TO 6

3 skinless, boneless chicken breasts, split in two
2 tablespoons sweet paprika
2 tablespoons corn, peanut, or vegetable oil
1/4 pound (1 stick) butter
2 tablespoons finely chopped shallots

1/2 cup cognac
2 cups orange juice
2 tablespoons arrowroot or cornstarch
salt and freshly ground pepper
chopped fresh parsley
orange peel in julienne strips (optional)

1. Trim away all traces of fat and membrane from chicken breasts. Wash and pat dry with paper towels. Sprinkle both sides with paprika.

2. In a 12-inch sauté pan, skillet, or heavy Dutch oven, heat oil and butter over moderate heat. When the foaming subsides,

add chicken breasts and sauté for about 5 minutes until golden. Turn and cook on the other side until done. Remove chicken to platter and keep warm.

3. Pour off and discard all but about 3 tablespoons fat from the pan. Add shallots and cook until soft but not brown.

4. Add cognac and stir to dissolve the brown particles clinging to the bottom and sides of the pan. Boil for a minute to reduce.

5. In a small bowl, combine orange juice and arrowroot or cornstarch, and mix until smooth. Add to the pan and continue to cook and stir until sauce is thickened. Add salt and pepper to taste.

6. Return chicken breasts to sauce and cook over moderate heat for 10 to 12 minutes, coating with sauce on both sides so that the breasts are shiny with glaze. Taste and correct seasoning. Transfer to heated serving platter. Sprinkle with chopped parsley. Pass extra sauce in gravy boat.

7. For the optional julienne of orange peel garnish, with a sharp knife or zester remove only the colored part of the peel of 1 or 2 oranges, avoiding the white pith, which is bitter. Cut into thin julienne strips about 2 inches long. Blanch in boiling water for 4 minutes. Drain well. Add to the skillet with the chicken breasts.

▨ Sautéed Breast of Chicken

These tender, succulent, lemon-scented chicken breast slices are frequently mistaken for veal. They can be made ahead and re-heated in the oven, but they are at their best when freshly cooked. Sweet and sour red cabbage and creamy mashed potatoes are good accompaniments.

SERVES 6 TO 8

4 whole chicken breasts, skinned and
  boned
salt and freshly ground pepper
1/2 cup flour
2 eggs
1/2 cup chopped fresh parsley

1 cup fine bread crumbs
1/3 cup grated Parmesan cheese
1/4 cup olive oil
1/4 cup (1/2 stick) butter
1/4 cup lemon juice
chopped fresh parsley

1. Cut chicken breasts in two. Trim all fat and membrane. Rinse and pat dry.

2. Place each half-breast between two sheets of wax paper, and with a flat mallet or cleaver pound until thin, taking care not to break the flesh. Cut each half-breast in two, giving you 16 pieces. Salt and pepper lightly.

3. Place flour on a square of wax paper. In a flat, shallow bowl, beat eggs and mix in parsley. Mix bread crumbs and Parmesan cheese, and spread on a square of wax paper, a little at a time so you don't dampen all the crumbs.

4. Dip chicken slices first in the flour, shaking off the excess, then in the egg mixture, allowing the excess to drain back into the bowl, and finally in the bread crumbs, patting them on to make them adhere.

5. Heat olive oil and butter in a large skillet. When the butter stops foaming, add the chicken slices, as many as will fit in the bottom of the pan without crowding. Sauté until golden, 3 to 4 minutes on each side. Keep the finished slices warm until all are done.

6. Add lemon juice to the skillet and stir over low heat to dissolve the brown particles clinging to the bottom and sides of the pan. Pour sauce over chicken fillets.

7. Remove to a warmed platter and sprinkle tops with parsley.

◈ Breast of Chicken with String Beans Vinaigrette

A fine luncheon or light supper dish.

SERVES 4 TO 6

4 whole chicken breasts with skin and
  bone
1 stalk celery
1 carrot, scraped and cut into
  quarters
1 small onion
4 cups chicken broth
1 pound tender young string beans

3/4 cup vinaigrette dressing
  (page 145)
1/4 cup pimientos, drained and
  chopped
Boston or Bibb lettuce
1 tablespoon minced fresh parsley
tomato wedges

1. Rinse chicken breasts and split in two. Place in a large pot with celery, carrot, onion, and chicken broth to cover. Poach chicken

with the pot partially covered, until chicken is tender, about 30 minutes. Remove the chicken and reserve the broth. Strain broth and return to pot.

2. Remove ends from string beans, leaving them whole. Place in boiling chicken broth and cook until just crisp-tender, 10 to 12 minutes. They should be bright green and crunchy. Drain and refresh under cold running water. Chill in the refrigerator.

3. When chicken is cool enough to handle, discard skin and remove meat from bone. Cut meat into cubes, toss with ¼ cup of vinaigrette, and refrigerate.

4. Toss string beans with remaining vinaigrette. Mix in pimientos and refrigerate.

5. When ready to serve, line a serving platter with lettuce and spread the string beans over. Mound chicken salad over beans and sprinkle with chopped parsley. Surround with tomato wedges.

⊠ Fried Buttermilk Chicken

SERVES 4 TO 6

2 3-pound frying chickens, cut into serving pieces
2 cups buttermilk
1 tablespoon paprika
few dashes of Tabasco sauce
½ teaspoon sage
½ cup finely chopped shallots
salt and freshly ground pepper
½ cup whole wheat flour
½ cup all-purpose flour
½ cup butter-flavored Crisco
½ cup regular Crisco

1. Wash chicken pieces, remove and discard skin, and trim away all strips of fat. Pat dry.

2. Mix together buttermilk, paprika, Tabasco sauce, sage, shallots, salt, and pepper in a shallow bowl.

3. Dip both sides of chicken pieces into buttermilk mixture.

4. Combine flours and spread on a sheet of wax paper.

5. Coat chicken with flour and place in a single layer on wax paper. Let stand at room temperature for 1 to 2 hours.

6. In a large skillet, heat fat to 365° on a frying thermometer or until a cube of bread browns in 60 seconds.

7. Submerge chicken pieces in hot fat, one at a time, without crowding. Cook 10 to 12 minutes on each side until brown and done, turning with kitchen tongs. Continue until all are done.

8. Drain on absorbent paper. Serve at room temperature.

◪ My Mother's Fried Chicken

The bacon flavor in the cooking fat adds an extra fillip of taste to this crisp, well-seasoned chicken. It is often used in regional southern cooking, but its inclusion is optional, according to your personal taste.

SERVES 8 OR MORE

2 3-pound chickens
2 teaspoons coarse salt, such as kosher
   salt
1 tablespoon freshly ground black
   pepper
1 teaspoon poultry seasoning
1 tablespoon sweet paprika
pinch of cayenne pepper

2 cups unbleached all-purpose flour
$^{1}/_{2}$ pound white shortening
$^{1}/_{2}$ pound pure lard (or increase the
   amount of white shortening by $^{1}/_{2}$
   pound)
2 or 3 tablespoons bacon fat
   (optional)

1. Cut each chicken into 8 pieces: 2 legs, 2 thighs, 2 breast pieces, 2 wings (with wing tips removed). Save the backbones, wing tips, and necks for some future stock making.

2. Combine salt, black pepper, poultry seasoning, paprika, and cayenne, and mix well. Coat chicken pieces with this mixture.

3. Place flour in a large, heavy, brown paper bag. Add chicken, a few pieces at a time, and toss. Remove and shake off excess flour.

4. Melt white shortening, lard, and bacon fat in a large skillet, preferably black iron. Heat the fat until it is lightly smoking.

5. Add chicken pieces, skin side up, and cook until crisp and golden brown on one side, about 12 to 14 minutes. Turn the pieces with kitchen tongs and continue cooking 12 to 14 minutes on the second side, taking care not to burn the pieces. As chicken pieces are done, keep them warm in a 250° oven while you fry the second batch.

▧ Butterflied Barbecued Baby Chickens

Use either 1-pound baby chickens or 1-pound Rock Cornish hens.

SERVES 4

BARBECUE SAUCE

1 cup very finely chopped green
   onions
1/4 cup honey
1/4 cup dark brown sugar
1/4 cup Worcestershire sauce
1 clove garlic, finely minced

1 tablespoon dry mustard
1 teaspoon chili powder
1 cup Sauternes or sweet white wine
1/4 cup sherry wine vinegar
salt and freshly ground pepper

4 1-pound chickens or Rock Cornish
   hens
1/2 cup (1 stick) butter

1. Combine all the barbecue sauce ingredients in a small sauce-pan and bring to a boil. Reduce heat and simmer for 10 minutes.

2. Wash chickens, pat dry, and trim fat from cavities. Place the bird breast side down. Using a kitchen shears or a sharp carving knife, cut along both sides of the backbone and remove. (Freeze the backbones and save for your next batch of chicken stock.)

3. Turn the bird breast side up and spread out the two halves. Pound the breastbone lightly so that the bird lies flat. Bend the wings and breast section toward you, breaking the shoulder bones. With a small pointed knife, cut a 3/4-inch gash in the lower skin area on both sides of the breast, near the soft cartilage. Lift a leg and tuck it through the gash, pulling the skin over the leg joint. Repeat with the other leg.

4. Coat the two sides of the birds generously with the sauce.

5. In a large skillet, heat butter until foaming. Place chickens skin side down in the hot fat and sauté for 15 to 20 minutes until golden. (This may be done hours ahead of serving time with the final baking left for the dinner hour.)

6. Preheat oven to 375°.

7. Transfer chickens to a baking pan skin side up. Bake 25 minutes longer or until tender. Baste with juices from time to time, adding more sauce if needed.

▨ Oven-barbecued Chicken

A no-fuss, no-muss chicken preparation that emerges from the oven brown and shiny with glaze and sparkling with flavor. The sauce may also be used with pork, meatballs, or beef pot roast. Store leftover sauce in a covered jar in the refrigerator.

SERVES 3 TO 4

BARBECUE SAUCE

3 tablespoons balsamic vinegar
1/2 cup sherry wine vinegar
1/4 cup dry sherry
1/4 cup (or more) honey
1 tablespoon Dijon mustard
1 teaspoon (or more) garlic Chili-paste*

1/2 teaspoon minced garlic
1 teaspoon celery seeds
1/2 tablespoon Worcestershire sauce
dash of Tabasco or hot pepper sauce
2 tablespoons Bovril**
salt and freshly ground pepper

3- to 3 1/2-pound broiler, cut into quarters
4 tablespoons (1/2 stick) butter

1. Grease a shallow baking pan large enough to hold the chicken in a single layer. Preheat oven to 400°.
2. Combine all barbecue sauce ingredients in a small bowl and blend well with a wire whisk. Taste for seasoning; you may want a bit more honey or hot Chilipaste.
3. Trim fat and excess skin from chicken quarters. Rinse chicken and pat dry.
4. Transfer chicken to baking pan and spoon both sides generously with barbecue sauce. Turn chicken pieces skin side down and dot with butter.
5. Bake 30 minutes on each side, basting with pan juices frequently and brushing with additional barbecue sauce if needed.
6. Transfer to a heated platter.

*Available in Oriental markets.
**Bovril is a beef-flavored, concentrated liquid bouillon, available in specialty food stores and some supermarkets.

⬛ Old-fashioned Chicken Pot Pie

Dinner guests have called this chicken pot pie spectacular. Don't let the seeming length of the recipe discourage you. While it is scarcely a 30-minute dish, many steps can be completed well in advance. You can prepare the chicken, the broth, and the pastry a day or even two ahead. At a busy time, I have even completed the pie the day before I planned to serve it, and the overnight stay in the refrigerator before baking does it no damage.

You can make it with fowl or roasting chicken, but capon is the bird of my choice. Capon is meaty and flavorful and will not fall apart even after long cooking. With a tossed green salad and miniature corn muffins, your guests will be served a feast.

SERVES 12 OR MORE

CRUST
4 cups sifted all-purpose flour
1 pound cold butter, cut into cubes

1¼ to 1½ cups ice water

CHICKEN AND BROTH
6- to 7-pound capon
8 cups chicken broth, fresh or canned
1 carrot, unpeeled and well-scrubbed
1 large whole onion, peeled

4 stalks celery, cut in two
4 sprigs parsley, Italian or curly
salt and pepper

PIE FILLING
cooked chicken, skinned and cut into
 substantial pieces
4 carrots, scraped, sliced in ½-inch
 rounds
½ pound string beans, broken into
 1-inch pieces
12 small white onions
4 stalks celery, cut in ½-inch slices

2 medium parsnips, scraped and cut
 in ½-inch rounds
2 medium potatoes, peeled and cut in
 1-inch cubes
10½-ounce package frozen green
 peas
4-ounce jar pimientos, well drained
 and diced

SAUCE
1 cup flour
¾ cup water
chicken broth

1 cup grated Parmesan cheese
1 cup heavy cream
salt and pepper

1. For the crust, place flour and butter in container of food processor, using the steel blade, and cover with the lid. Process, turning on and off rapidly, until butter is cut into flour and the mixture is crumbly; do not overprocess. Add ice water and process, turning on and off a few times, just until dough begins to mass together. Remove dough from processor, gather into a ball, and flatten slightly. Flour it lightly, cover tightly with plastic wrap, and refrigerate until ready to use.

2. If you do not use a food processor, place flour in a mixing bowl. Add butter and cut it in with a pastry blender or two knives until it looks like coarse cornmeal. Sprinkle water over flour mixture and toss with a fork until dough begins to mass together. Gather into a ball and proceed as above.

3. To prepare broth, place chicken in a large kettle with chicken broth, carrot, onion, celery, and parsley. The liquid should completely cover the ingredients. Add more water or broth if needed. Cover pot and bring slowly to a boil.

4. Reduce heat and tilt cover so that there is an inch or so of open space. Skim the surface of the soup at frequent intervals, until the scum changes to a white foam, at which point you can ignore it as it slowly cooks. Simmer for about 1 hour or until the bird is tender and the juices at the thigh joint run clear when pierced with a fork.

5. Remove chicken from pot and let cool.

6. Strain broth and discard vegetables. Season to taste with salt and pepper. With a large spoon, skim the fat on the surface of the broth. If possible, let broth cool, cover with plastic wrap, and refrigerate for a few hours or overnight, making the removal of the fat simpler and more efficient.

7. When chicken is cool enough to handle, remove and discard skin and cut meat into substantial pieces. Set aside.

8. For the pie filling, cook sliced carrots, string beans, white onions, celery, parsnips, and potatoes in broth, covered, for 9 to 10 minutes, or until barely tender. Add green peas a minute before vegetables finish cooking, just long enough to thaw them.

9. Strain broth and return to pot. Reserve vegetables. Cook broth over moderately high heat for about 30 minutes to reduce. You should have about 8 cups.

10. Add pimientos to vegetables and mix through.

11. Lightly oil an ovenproof baking dish that measures about 14 by 11 inches and is 2 inches deep.

12. Spread cut-up chicken over bottom of baking dish. Cover with cooked vegetables.

13. For the sauce, mix flour and water in a small bowl until smooth. Slowly stir into hot chicken broth and cook over moderate heat, whisking with a wire whisk until sauce is thickened and smooth, the consistency of heavy cream. Stir in grated Parmesan cheese and heavy cream. Heat through, but do not allow to boil. Taste for seasoning, and add salt and pepper as needed.

14. Ladle sauce over chicken and vegetables to the top of the baking dish. You will need about 7 cups of sauce. Sprinkle with freshly ground black pepper. Let mixture cool completely before covering with crust.

15. Roll out pastry on a lightly floured surface to a thickness of ⅜ to ½ inch and large enough to fit the baking dish with a generous 1-inch overlap all around.

16. Cover the cooled filling with the crust. Roll back the edges and crimp with the tines of a fork to make it adhere tightly to the edge of the baking dish. Cut vents in the crust or prick with a fork to allow steam to escape. If possible, refrigerate the pie for 1 hour or longer before baking.

17. Preheat oven to 400°.

18. Place baking dish on aluminum foil or a baking sheet to catch the juices that may bubble over. Bake for 20 minutes and reduce heat to 375°. Bake an additional 35 to 40 minutes or until the crust is nicely browned and cooked through.

▨ Summer Chicken

Chicken crowned with a mélange of summertime vegetables. It can be made a day ahead and reheated or served at room temperature.

SERVES 4 TO 6

VEGETABLE TOPPING*

1/4 cup olive oil
2 medium onions, finely chopped
2 stalks celery, cut in 1/4-inch dice
2 cloves garlic, finely minced
1 green pepper, cut in 1/4-inch dice
1 red pepper, cut in 1/4-inch dice
1 medium eggplant, unpeeled, cut in 1/4-inch dice (remove heavily seeded portions)

1 small zucchini, unpeeled, cut in 1/4-inch dice
1 small yellow squash, unpeeled, cut in 1/4-inch dice
1 1-pound can peeled tomatoes, crushed and undrained
1 teaspoon dried oregano
1 teaspoon dried rosemary, crushed
salt and freshly ground pepper

2 2 1/2- to 3-pound broilers
salt and freshly ground pepper

4 tablespoons (1/2 stick) butter
1/4 cup corn, vegetable, or peanut oil

1. In a 12-inch skillet or sauté pan with a cover, heat olive oil. Add chopped onions and celery, and cook until onions are soft but not brown, about 10 minutes, stirring often.

2. Add minced garlic, all the vegetables, and the herbs. Cook covered, stirring from time to time, until eggplant is soft, 25 to 30 minutes. Season to taste with salt and pepper. If there seems to be too much liquid, cook uncovered until thickened.

3. Transfer cooked vegetables to a bowl and keep warm.

4. Cut each chicken into 8 serving pieces. Season lightly with salt and pepper.

5. Using the same skillet, heat butter and oil until butter stops foaming.

6. Add chicken pieces, large ones first, without crowding, and cook until nicely brown, 10 to 12 minutes. Turn pieces with kitchen tongs and cook the other side 10 to 12 minutes longer, until done. You may have to brown the chicken in batches. As pieces are done, remove them to a platter and keep warm.

7. When all the chicken is cooked, return to skillet, cover generously with vegetables, and heat thoroughly for 10 minutes longer.

*You will not need all the vegetable topping. Use the leftover at another meal as a cold appetizer or heated as a vegetable side dish.

⊠ Roast Capon with Rosemary Butter

SERVES 6

6- to 7-pound capon, cleaned and
    dressed
1 tablespoon dried rosemary,
    crumbled
6 tablespoons (³/₄ stick) soft butter

salt and freshly ground pepper
1 cup chopped onions
2 stalks celery, coarsely chopped
1 large carrot, coarsely chopped
2 cups chicken broth, fresh or canned

1. Preheat oven to 500°.

2. Rinse bird inside and out and pat dry. Remove clumps of fat from the crop and cavity.

3. Blend rosemary, butter, salt, and pepper into a paste. Rub over the outside and inside of the bird.

4. Spread chopped onions, celery, and carrot over bottom of a shallow baking pan.

5. Place bird on the bed of vegetables breast side up. Bake for 1 hour, without opening the oven door. To test for doneness, cut a deep slit between the leg and the body. If the juices run clear without a tinge of red, the bird is done. If not, return to oven for an additional 10 minutes or so. Remove cooked capon to a platter and keep warm.

6. Place the roasting pan on top of the stove. Add chicken broth and bring to a boil, while scraping the bottom of the pan with a wooden spoon to gather up all the juices. Cook rapidly until the sauce is reduced by half. Strain sauce and serve separately in a sauceboat.

⊠ Squabs with Bacon

SERVES 4 TO 6

12 squabs, cleaned and dressed
1/2 cup cognac
1/2 cup flour
salt and freshly ground pepper
1 pound lean bacon (place in freezer
   for easy cutting)

1 onion, finely chopped
2 stalks celery, finely chopped
3 cups chicken broth, fresh or canned

1. Rub inside and outside of squabs with cognac, reserving 1 tablespoon for gravy. Dust birds with flour and sprinkle lightly with salt and pepper.

2. Chop bacon in small dice. In a baking pan or casserole large enough to hold squabs in a single layer, fry bacon until crisp. Remove bacon with a slotted spoon and drain on paper towels.

3. Place squabs in bacon fat and brown nicely on all sides. Turn the birds breast side down in the baking pan and add onion, celery, and chicken broth. Cover pan tightly — aluminum foil will do if there isn't a cover — and simmer slowly for 1 1/2 hours, or until tender.

4. Remove to a warm serving platter when done and sprinkle generously with bacon bits.

5. Cook sauce over brisk heat until reduced. Add the reserved tablespoon cognac. Taste for seasoning and correct. Serve gravy separately in a gravy boat.

⊠ Roast Quail

SERVES 3

6 quail
1/2 cup whole wheat flour
salt and freshly ground pepper
1 teaspoon sage
1/4 pound (1 stick) butter

1 cup finely chopped shallots
1 bay leaf
1 cup Sauternes wine
watercress

1. Preheat oven to 375°.

2. Rinse birds and wipe dry.

3. Mix together flour, salt, pepper, and sage. Dredge birds in seasoned flour.

4. In a large skillet, melt butter. Add quail and brown well on all sides. Remove browned birds to a baking pan and set aside.

5. Add shallots to skillet, and cook and toss until limp. Add bay leaf and Sauternes, bring to a boil, and simmer for 2 minutes, scraping up any browned bits on bottom of pan.

6. Pour sauce over quail in baking pan and bake, uncovered, for 45 to 50 minutes, or until tender. Baste frequently; quail tend to be dry and need frequent basting.

7. Transfer quail to a warm platter and pour remaining drippings over birds. Garnish platter generously with crisp watercress.

▦ Roast Duck

SERVES 2 TO 4

5- to 6-pound duck
1 clove garlic, crushed and minced
salt and freshly ground pepper
1 teaspoon ground ginger
1 lemon
coarse salt and freshly ground pepper

1 orange
1 cup chicken broth
1 tablespoon cornstarch or arrowroot
1/2 cup orange juice
1/4 cup Grand Marnier

1. Wash duck and cut away excess fat at cavities. Dry thoroughly.

2. Combine garlic, salt, pepper, and ginger. Rub cavity of duck with mixture.

3. Prick skin of duck with the tines of a fork. Cut lemon in half and rub the duck all over, squeezing the lemon as you go. Sprinkle with coarse salt and pepper.

4. Cut orange into quarters and place inside cavity.

5. Let duck stand at room temperature for 1 hour.

6. Preheat oven to 450°.

7. Place duck on a rack in a shallow roasting pan and roast for 1 1/2 hours. Prick the skin and turn the bird from time to time.

8. Pour off fat, pour chicken broth over the bird, and continue roasting for 1 additional hour.

9. Remove duck to a platter and keep warm.

10. Spoon off fat from gravy. Add cornstarch or arrowroot to the pan juices and stir until smooth. Add orange juice and Grand Marnier, and warm through. Taste and correct seasonings. Strain gravy into sauceboat and serve with duck, cut into quarters or halves.

⊠ Roast Goose

A traditional Christmas bird.

SERVES 4 TO 6

24 pitted prunes, largest size
1 cup Armagnac
9- to 10-pound goose, cleaned and
dressed
1½ cups water
2 tablespoons fresh lemon juice
1 clove garlic, minced
2 tablespoons coarse salt

freshly ground pepper
1 cup chicken broth
1 onion, coarsely chopped
1 stalk celery, coarsely chopped
1 carrot, coarsely chopped
1 clove garlic, minced
2 tablespoons flour

1. The night before you cook the goose, soak prunes in Armagnac in a small bowl, covered with plastic wrap. Do not refrigerate.

2. When ready to cook, preheat oven to 450°.

3. Rinse goose and pat dry. Trim away fat from cavities. Reserve giblets.

4. In a small saucepan, combine water with the goose giblets, liver, and neck. Bring to a boil, reduce heat, and simmer gently to make a stock for the gravy.

5. Rub inside and outside of goose with lemon juice. Rub cavity with minced garlic and sprinkle bird with salt and pepper. Prick skin all over with the tines of a fork. Stuff cavity with prunes and fasten cavity closed with skewers.

6. Place goose on a rack in a shallow roasting pan and roast for 25 minutes, pouring off fat as it accumulates.

7. Lower heat to 350°. Add chicken broth, onion, celery, carrot, and garlic to baking pan. Bake 1½ to 2 hours longer, or until crisp and tender.

8. When goose is done, remove to a serving platter and keep warm.

9. Skim fat from gravy. Strain giblet stock. Dissolve flour in stock and add to pan drippings, stirring well. Strain gravy. Taste for seasonings and correct. Pass gravy separately in gravy boat.

Marinated Roast Turkey

No longer do we think of turkey only when the frost is on the pumpkin. With improved barnyard technology, fresh-killed birds are available the year round, and fine they are for a buffet or a large gathering. Here is a different and provocatively flavored version, to be served at room temperature.

SERVES 10

MARINADE

2 cups soy sauce
2 bay leaves, crumbled
1 tablespoon dried rosemary, crushed
1 cup sherry wine vinegar
1 cup dry white wine
1 cup honey
6 juniper berries, crushed
freshly ground pepper
1 tablespoon poultry seasoning
1 large onion, coarsely chopped
3 cloves garlic, crushed

12- to 15-pound turkey, cleaned and dressed
3 tablespoons butter
3 tablespoons peanut oil
3 tablespoons olive oil

1. Combine all marinade ingredients in a large saucepan and bring to a boil. Boil for 5 minutes. Cool completely.

2. Place turkey in a heavy-duty plastic bag. Add the marinade. Close bag tightly, securing well. Place bag on a platter as a precaution against an unexpected leak and refrigerate for 24 hours, turning the bag a few times so that all parts of the bird will be awash in the marinade.

3. A few hours before roasting, remove turkey from marinade and let it come to room temperature.

4. Preheat oven to 350°.

5. Pat bird dry with paper towels. Rub with butter and a mixture of the peanut and olive oils.

6. Place turkey on a rack in a roasting pan, breast side down. Roast for 15 minutes to the pound, 3 to 4 hours. For the last 45 minutes of roasting, turn the bird breast side up. To test for doneness, cut a deep slit between the leg and the body. If the juices run clear, without a tinge of red, the bird is done. Throughout the baking, baste with the marinade every 20 minutes. If the skin gets too dark, cover with aluminum foil, continuing to baste. Let the bird rest at least 30 minutes after being removed from the oven, before carving.

⊠ Granny's Light Bread Stuffing

Granny Dameron never used the term "white bread": she called it "light bread" or "loaf bread." This was her favorite summertime poultry stuffing. It is airy and light — perhaps because it's made of light bread? I make it with Pepperidge Farm white bread, which works very well and needs no toasting, an added bonus for a busy cook.

MAKES ENOUGH FOR A
5- TO 6-POUND BIRD

3 cups "light bread" cubes
¼ pound (1 stick) butter
½ cup coarsely chopped celery

½ cup coarsely chopped onions
salt and freshly ground pepper

1. Trim crusts from bread and cut bread into ⅜-inch cubes. Set aside.
2. In a large skillet, heat butter and sauté celery and onions until wilted. Do not brown.
3. Add bread cubes and toss well, until bread cubes are golden.
4. Taste for seasoning and add salt and pepper as needed.
5. Rub a 5- to 6-pound roasting chicken or capon with coarse salt and pepper; fill cavity three-quarters full with stuffing. Sew bird closed or close with skewers.

⊠ Apple Cornbread Stuffing

MAKES ENOUGH FOR A
LARGE TURKEY OR CAPON

1 pound loose pork sausage meat
2 cups finely chopped onions
2 cups finely chopped celery
1/2 cup finely chopped green bell
*   pepper*
1/2 cup finely chopped red bell pepper
4 cups crumbled cornbread
*   (page 171)*
4 cups fresh white bread crumbs (8 to
*   10 slices)*

2 tablespoons sage
1 tablespoon dried thyme
1/4 cup finely chopped parsley
2 tart apples (Granny Smith), peeled,
*   cored, and coarsely chopped*
1/4 pound (1 stick) melted butter
1 cup chicken broth
1/2 cup dry vermouth
salt and freshly ground pepper

1. Place sausage meat in a large skillet and cook until it loses its raw look. Add onions, celery, and green and red peppers, and cook until vegetables are limp. Do not drain.

2. In a large bowl, combine crumbled cornbread, bread crumbs, sage, thyme, parsley, and apples. Add melted butter and toss.

3. Add sausage mixture, chicken broth, and dry vermouth. Toss well. Add salt and pepper to taste. Add additional chicken broth if the mixture seems too dry.

4. Fill bird three-quarters full with stuffing, and sew bird closed or close with skewers. Place leftover dressing in a buttered casserole, cover, and bake along with the bird in a 350° oven for the last 45 or 50 minutes that the bird is in the oven.

⊠ Apple, Prune, and Chestnut Stuffing

A favorite stuffing for the big bird at holiday time.

MAKES ENOUGH FOR A
12- TO 15-POUND TURKEY

4 cups fresh bread crumbs
2 cups chopped tart apples (preferably
  Granny Smith)
1/2 pound chicken livers
1/2 cup (1 stick) butter
1/2 cup finely chopped shallots
1/2 cup coarsely chopped celery
1/3 cup chopped parsley

1 tablespoon sage
1 tablespoon dried thyme
1 1/2 cups pitted prunes, coarsely
  chopped
1 cup chopped chestnuts
1 cup dry white wine
chicken broth (if needed)
salt and freshly ground pepper

1. Prepare fresh bread crumbs with sliced white bread in blender or food processor with the steel blade in position. Set crumbs aside.

2. Peel and core apples. Chop coarsely and set aside.

3. Pick over chicken livers, trimming away membranes and tabs of fat.

4. Melt butter in a large skillet. Add chopped shallots, celery, and chicken livers. Toss and sauté until the pink disappears from livers. Remove livers with a slotted spoon to a wooden bowl or board, and chop coarsely. Return to skillet and toss with shallots and celery.

5. Add to liver mixture the apples, parsley, sage, thyme, prunes, and chestnuts, and blend well. Mix in white wine. Add chicken broth if the mixture seems dry. Season to taste with salt and pepper.

6. Just before roasting, stuff bird. The bread crumbs will swell, so fill the bird no more than three-quarters full. Sew the body cavity closed or close with skewers. Leftover stuffing can be placed in a greased casserole and baked, covered, with the bird in a 350° oven for the last 45 or 50 minutes of baking.

Fish
and
Shellfish

▨ Stuffed Baked Brook Trout

Brook trout has always been a popular fish that I stuff and wrap in bacon, making it even more delectable.

SERVES 6

6 medium brook trout
4 tablespoons (½ stick) butter
1 cup finely chopped mushrooms
½ cup finely chopped onions
¼ cup finely chopped celery
¼ cup finely chopped green pepper

¼ cup finely chopped red pepper
½ cup bread crumbs, lightly toasted
salt and freshly ground pepper
12 slices lean bacon
½ cup dry white wine

1. Have your fish man clean and gut the fish, leaving it whole but removing the bone. Do not have the head removed; the flesh is juicier if the head is not removed. Wash the fish and pat dry. Set aside.

2. Preheat oven to 400°.

3. Heat butter in a medium-size skillet and sauté all the vegetables until tender.

4. Add bread crumbs and mix.

5. Season stuffing with salt and pepper.

6. Blanch bacon strips in boiling water for 2 or 3 minutes. Drain and dry thoroughly on paper towels.

7. Fill each fish cavity with about 2 tablespoons of stuffing.

8. Wrap each fish with 2 slices of bacon.

9. Place stuffed fish in a greased flat baking pan.

10. Add white wine to skillet and stir to dissolve brown particles clinging to the bottom and sides of the pan. Boil a few minutes to reduce sauce. Pour over fish.

11. Bake for 20 to 25 minutes, or until fish loses its translucency.

◈ Crab Cakes

Accompany with a baked potato and coleslaw for a splendid meal.

SERVES 3

1 pound fresh lump crabmeat
1/2 cup seasoned Italian bread crumbs
1/2 to 3/4 cup mayonnaise
1 egg, lightly beaten
1 teaspoon Worcestershire sauce
1 tablespoon prepared horseradish
1 teaspoon lemon juice

1/2 teaspoon dry mustard
salt and freshly ground pepper
additional bread crumbs for coating
6 tablespoons clarified butter
   (page 162)
lemon wedges
tartar sauce (page 160)

1. Pick over crabmeat to remove pieces of shell. Set aside.
2. In a medium-size bowl, combine bread crumbs, mayonnaise, egg, Worcestershire sauce, horseradish, lemon juice, and mustard, and mix well.
3. Add bread crumb mixture to crabmeat and blend lightly. Season with salt and pepper.
4. Form into 6 cakes.
5. Sprinkle a square of wax paper with bread crumbs and coat both sides of crab cakes thickly.
6. In a large skillet, heat clarified butter and sauté cakes until golden, 3 to 4 minutes on each side.
7. Serve with lemon wedges and tartar sauce.

◈ Fish Mousse with Hollandaise Sauce

SERVES 4 TO 6

1 tablespoon soft butter
1 pound fillets of white fish (floun-
   der, sole, cod)
3 egg whites
1 cup heavy cream, or more

salt and freshly ground pepper
dash of cayenne pepper
hollandaise sauce (page 160)
cooked shrimps

1. Butter 4 to 6 individual molds with softened butter.
2. Using the steel blade in the food processor, grind fish to a fine puree. Add egg whites and cream, and process until completely smooth. Blend in salt, pepper, and cayenne pepper.

3. Transfer puree to a bowl, place the bowl in a larger one filled with cracked ice, and refrigerate for 1 hour.

4. Preheat oven to 350°.

5. Stir mixture thoroughly and spoon into buttered molds. Cover each with a sheet of buttered wax paper or aluminum foil and place in a baking pan in the lowest third of the oven. Pour in enough boiling water to come halfway up the sides of the molds and bake for about 20 minutes or until firm.

6. Remove from oven and discard the paper covering. Invert each mold on a serving plate, and turn out the mousse.

7. Spoon hollandaise sauce over each and garnish with cooked shrimps. Steamed rice is a suitable accompaniment.

▨ Pan-fried Porgies

The church social looms large in my book of childhood memories. It had a noble purpose: to raise funds for a new furnace and the coal to stoke it with so that the parishioners would be warm on Sunday mornings, or perhaps for new shingles for the roof so we would be dry. However, I was far more interested in the *modus operandi* of raising the funds since most of it centered around food. There were all kinds of mouth-watering treats to buy and eat. Still vivid in my mind are the fried porgies that Miss Inez Corell produced with clocklike regularity year after year in her huge black iron wash pot. We'll do them in a skillet.

SERVES 6

6 medium-size porgies, split and filleted
salt and freshly ground pepper
1 cup stone ground cornmeal

1 cup corn, peanut, or other vegetable oil
lemon wedges

1. Rinse fillets, but do not dry.

2. Sprinkle with salt and a few grinds of pepper.

3. Spread cornmeal on a square of wax paper and dredge both sides of fillets in cornmeal, covering them generously. (Use a small amount of cornmeal at a time so that you don't dampen all of it.)

4. Place fillets on a sheet of wax paper in one layer and let stand at room temperature for 30 minutes.

5. Heat oil in a large skillet over moderate heat and cook fish for 2 to 3 minutes on each side. Don't cook more at a time than will fit in a single layer without crowding. As they are done, drain on absorbent paper towels.

6. Transfer to platter and garnish with lemon wedges.

⊠ Salmon Trout Dumplings with Hollandaise Sauce

Granny Dameron's repertoire of dumplings was impressive; she could transform undistinguished chunks of fish, poultry, or veal into airy morsels that seemed ready to float off the plate. Picture my surprise, then, when I first visited France to learn that Granny's dumplings were the mysterious and highly regarded *quenelles*, which are simply patties made with uncooked fish or meat and poached. Food processors and blenders have greatly simplified a procedure that in Granny Dameron's day required laborious sessions with a meat grinder and lots of arm power and patience.

A stream that flowed near Granny's house abounded with salmon trout from which she produced what we children identified as "pink dumplings," but any kind of white fish fillets may be substituted in the recipe that follows.

MAKES ABOUT 20, SERVING 6 FOR
LUNCH OR 10 AS A FIRST COURSE

2 pounds boneless and skinless salmon trout fillets or any white fish fillets
2 whole eggs
2 egg whites

2 cups heavy cream
1/2 teaspoon grated nutmeg
salt and freshly ground pepper
hollandaise sauce (page 160)*

1. With the metal blade in place, place fish cut in 1-inch pieces in the container of food processor. Process, turning on and off rapidly until a smooth puree is formed.

2. Add eggs, egg whites, cream, nutmeg, salt, and pepper. Blend thoroughly until smooth.

*The hollandaise sauce may be further enriched by adding 1/4 cup champagne and 1/2 cup heavy cream, whipped.

3. Transfer to a bowl, and cover and refrigerate for 1 or 2 hours before shaping.

4. Roll small portions of the mixture between two large soup spoons, making a neat, egg-shaped nugget. Place each nugget on the bottom of a buttered skillet, close together. Ladle boiling salted water over them to barely cover, and cover with a round of wax paper cut to fit the inside of the skillet.

5. Bring to a boil. Reduce heat and simmer slowly — do not boil — for about 10 minutes, depending on size, until they are firm. Lift the paper after the first 5 minutes and gently turn each nugget with a rubber spatula.

6. Remove pan from heat and let stand for a minute or two. Drain the dumplings on paper towels and arrange on a heated serving dish.

7. Serve with hollandaise sauce.

▨ Bay Scallops in Mustard-Shallot Sauce

Tender, succulent bay scallops in a puddle of savory, mustard-scented sauce. Serve in small shells if used as an appetizer.

SERVES 4 TO 6 AS A MAIN COURSE,
8 AS AN APPETIZER

SAUCE
1 tablespoon butter
1/4 cup finely chopped shallots
2 tablespoons Dijon mustard

1/4 cup dry white wine
1/2 cup heavy cream
salt and pepper, if desired

2 pounds bay scallops
paprika
salt and freshly ground pepper

1/4 cup (1/2 stick) melted butter
1/4 cup chopped parsley
lemon wedges

1. For the sauce, melt butter in a small, nonaluminum saucepan. Add chopped shallots, and cook and stir until soft but not brown.

2. Stir in mustard and white wine until blended. Add heavy cream and stir until sauce becomes thickened, but do not boil. If sauce becomes too thick, thin with a bit of cream. Season with salt and pepper if desired. Set sauce aside and keep warm.

3. Rinse scallops and dry well on paper towels. Sprinkle generously with paprika, and salt and pepper if desired.

4. Heat butter in a small pan until melted.

5. Heat a large skillet over high heat until smoking. Add melted butter and scallops. Cook scallops for 2 to 3 minutes, shaking the pan so they will cook on all sides. Do not overcook or they will toughen. They are done the moment they become opaque.

6. Pour a layer of hot mustard-shallot sauce over the bottom of shells or serving dish. Remove scallops from skillet with a slotted spoon and place in the sauce. Sprinkle with chopped parsley and serve with lemon wedges.

⊠ Shad Roe Soufflé

Granny Dameron called this Shad Pudding, but since I have added to the number of eggs in the original recipe, it earns the right to be called a soufflé. Accompanied by grilled tomatoes and a mixed green salad, it makes a fine main course for a spring luncheon or a light supper.

SERVES 4

1/3 cup water
1/3 cup dry white wine
1 teaspoon lemon juice
4 pairs of shad roe (about 4 cups)
6 tablespoons (3/4 stick) butter
1/2 cup chopped shallots

6 tablespoons all-purpose flour
salt and freshly ground pepper
1 1/2 cups milk
6 large eggs, separated
2 tablespoons grated Parmesan cheese

1. In a medium-size, nonaluminum saucepan, combine water, wine, and lemon juice, and bring to a boil.

2. Reduce heat, add shad roe, cover pan, and steam until the roe loses its redness. When done, remove roe from pan and let cool. Discard liquid.

3. When cool enough to handle, peel off membranes from roe and set roe aside.

4. In saucepan, melt butter. Add shallots and sauté until just limp. Do not brown.

5. Stir in flour, salt, and pepper, and whisk over moderate heat until bubbly. Add milk and continue to cook and whisk over moderate heat until sauce is thickened and smooth.

6. Stir in shad roe and mix well. Remove from heat.

7. Separate eggs, placing whites in a large bowl. Lightly beat yolks.

8. Preheat oven to 350°. Place baking rack in lower third of oven. Butter a 2-quart soufflé dish and sprinkle bottom and sides with grated Parmesan cheese. Set aside.

9. When shad roe mixture is cooled, stir in beaten egg yolks and mix well.

10. With clean dry beaters, beat egg whites until stiff but not dry. Fold gently into shad roe mixture and blend until no white streaks remain.

11. Gently pour mixture into soufflé dish. Bake for 50 to 55 minutes, or until top is puffy and brown. Serve at once with lemon-dill butter (below).

Lemon-Dill Butter

¹/₄ pound (1 stick) soft butter
1 tablespoon lemon juice
1¹/₂ teaspoons grated lemon rind

2 teaspoons chopped fresh chives
2 teaspoons chopped fresh dill

1. In container of a food processor with the steel blade in place, process butter, lemon juice, and lemon rind, using a few on-and-off turns, until combined.

2. Transfer to a heatproof bowl and place over simmering water until the butter melts.

3. Mix in chopped chives and chopped dill, and serve warm over soufflé.

⊠ Sautéed Swordfish Steak

I have found that swordfish sometimes becomes dried out when broiled, but this method of cooking is unfailingly successful. The fish is juicy and delicious — exactly as it ought to be.

SERVES 4

4 swordfish steaks, ¹/₂ inch thick
  (about 2 pounds)
1 teaspoon salt
freshly ground black pepper
2 teaspoons sweet paprika
1 teaspoon ground or crushed fennel
  seeds

4 tablespoons (¹/₂ stick) butter
¹/₄ cup vegetable oil
1 tablespoon lemon juice
chopped fresh parsley

1. Wipe fish and dry well.
2. Mix together salt, pepper, paprika, and crushed or ground fennel seeds.
3. Rub both sides of fish with mixture.
4. In a skillet large enough to hold the fish steaks in a single layer, heat butter and oil over moderate heat until butter stops foaming.
5. Add fish and cook undisturbed for 7 to 8 minutes on each side, or until fish loses its translucency. Remove to platter.
6. Add lemon juice to skillet and stir to dissolve the brown particles clinging to the bottom and sides of the pan.
7. Pour pan drippings over fish steaks.
8. Sprinkle with chopped parsley and serve at once.

Vegetables

String Beans and New Potatoes

When I was a small boy in North Carolina, my springtime euphoria was heightened not only by the colorful masses of daffodils, tulips, sweet peas, and the like that surrounded our house, but also by the freshly harvested little red new potatoes that appeared often on the dinner table. They were shiny with melted butter and crowned with a sprinkling of either chopped fresh dill or parsley and coarse salt. These days, I accompany them with crisp fresh string beans.

SERVES 6 TO 8

16 to 20 small red new potatoes
2 pounds crisp fresh string beans
3 to 4 cups chicken broth, fresh or canned
pinch of salt
3 tablespoons melted butter
coarse salt (kosher salt)
3 tablespoons chopped fresh parsley

1. Scrub potatoes and peel a thin strip, about 1/4 inch, around the center, leaving the rest of the skin intact.
2. Wash string beans, drain, and snap off tips.
3. In a large saucepan, bring chicken broth to a boil. Add potatoes and pinch of salt. Cover pot and cook for 10 minutes.
4. Add string beans, cover pot, and continue to cook for 10 minutes, or until string beans are crisp-tender.
5. Drain vegetables and reserve cooking liquid for future stocks.
6. Toss potatoes and string beans with melted butter.
7. Transfer to a heated bowl and sprinkle with coarse salt and chopped parsley.

Bacon-wrapped String Beans

Individual servings of string beans and bacon cooked in a seasoned broth.

SERVES 6 TO 8

3 cups chicken broth, fresh or canned
1 carrot, sliced
1 onion, sliced
1 stalk celery, cut in thirds
1 pound crisp young string beans
9 or 10 slices lean bacon
salt and pepper if needed

1. In a large saucepan or 12-inch skillet with a cover, combine chicken broth, carrot, onion, and celery. Cover, bring to a boil, and boil gently for 30 minutes.

2. While the broth is cooking, wash string beans and break off ends. Make individual bundles of 6 string beans, each wrapped with a strip of bacon covering as much of the length of the beans as possible. The bacon will stick to itself and does not need strings or toothpicks.

3. Trim ends of beans that protrude beyond bacon. (Reserve the bits and pieces of beans for soup stock or perhaps a munch for the cook.)

4. Strain broth and discard vegetables. Return broth to saucepan or skillet and bring to a boil. Add a few grinds of black pepper and taste for seasoning. If broth is sufficiently seasoned, chances are you won't need additional salt.

5. Place string bean bundles in broth, cover pan, and cook gently for 20 minutes. If you need more liquid, add more broth or water.

6. Using kitchen tongs, remove bundles from broth and serve hot.

▨ Lima Beans in Sour Cream–Dill Sauce

SERVES 4 TO 5

3 pounds fresh baby lima beans
(about 3 cups shelled) or 1½
10-ounce packages frozen baby
lima beans
chicken broth

2 tablespoons melted butter
5 tablespoons sour cream
1 teaspoon lemon juice
2 tablespoons finely chopped fresh dill
salt and freshly ground pepper

1. Cut off the rounded edge of the lima beans and shell like peas. Pick them over carefully, and discard any that appear discolored or wormy. (If using frozen, cook according to package directions, using chicken broth in place of water.)

2. Pour about 3 inches of chicken broth into a heavy saucepan with a tightly fitting lid. Cover, and bring to a boil.

3. Add beans, cover tightly, and steam gently for 15 to 25 minutes, or until beans are tender. Time will vary depending on size and freshness, but do not overcook. Beans should be tender but offer the slightest suggestion of resistance when tasted.

4. Drain thoroughly (reserving the broth for your next pot of

soup) and return beans to saucepan. Shake well over low heat to get rid of all moisture.

5. In a small bowl, combine melted butter, sour cream, lemon juice, chopped dill, and salt and pepper to taste. Mix well.

6. Add sauce to beans in pot and toss well. Do not allow the sauce to boil or it will curdle. Transfer to a heated bowl and serve immediately.

▨ Beets Filled with Peas

An eye-filling cold side dish.

SERVES 6 TO 8

6 to 8 medium-size beets
2 tablespoons sugar
1 tablespoon salt
1/4 cup salad oil
1/4 cup sherry wine vinegar
1 10-ounce package frozen green
   peas

1/4 cup mayonnaise
1 teaspoon Dijon mustard
1/4 cup finely chopped shallots
1 teaspoon sour cream
salt and freshly ground pepper
red-edged leaf lettuce or Boston
   lettuce

1. Rinse beets gently, leaving about 2 inches of the tops and root ends.

2. Bring 8 cups of water to a boil, adding 1 tablespoon sugar and 1 tablespoon salt.

3. Add beets, cover the pot, and simmer slowly until tender. This may take anywhere from 30 minutes to 1 hour or more, depending on the age of the beets.

4. When tender, run under cold water and slip off skins. Cool.

5. With a melon ball scoop, remove the center of the beets and save for another use.

6. Mix salad oil, vinegar, and remaining tablespoon of sugar, and pour over beets. Marinate in refrigerator for a few hours.

7. Cook peas according to package directions. Drain and refresh under cold running water. Cool completely.

8. In a small bowl, mix together mayonnaise, mustard, shallots, and sour cream. Season with salt and pepper. Toss with peas.

9. Fill marinated beet cups.

10. Serve on a bed of red-edged leaf lettuce or Boston lettuce cups.

⬛ Baked Broccoli with Almonds

SERVES 6

1 large bunch broccoli (about
    2 pounds)
¹/₂ cup sliced almonds

2 cups béchamel sauce (page 159)
1 cup grated sharp cheddar cheese

1. Wash broccoli and cut into flowerets, leaving about 3 inches of stem. Peel away the tough outer skin of stems with a vegetable peeler.

2. Boil flowerets in a large quantity of salted water for 3 minutes. Plunge into cold water to stop the cooking and set the color. Drain and set aside.

3. Spread sliced almonds on a flat pan and toast in a 325° oven for 10 to 15 minutes until almonds are golden but not brown. Watch them carefully so that they don't get too dark.

4. Increase oven temperature to 350°. Butter an ovenproof baking dish about 7 by 10 inches and 3 inches deep.

5. Place a layer of broccoli flowerets over bottom of dish; cover with half the sauce; sprinkle half the almonds over sauce. Repeat second layer with flowerets, sauce, and almonds. Sprinkle top with grated cheese.

6. Bake in preheated oven for 30 to 40 minutes, or until cheese is melted and sauce bubbly.

⬛ Brussels Sprouts and Chestnuts

Perhaps it was the years of poor preparation that were responsible for brussels sprouts' somewhat tarnished reputation. However, properly cooked, they are crisp, well-flavored, and highly inviting, as illustrated in this recipe. Peak season for sprouts is from October through December.

SERVES 8

2 pounds brussels sprouts
1 cup finely chopped shallots
6 tablespoons (3/4 stick) butter
2 cups whole chestnuts (fresh or canned, not in syrup)

1 teaspoon lemon juice
salt and freshly ground pepper
1 tablespoon chopped fresh dill
1/2 cup dry bread crumbs browned in 2 tablespoons butter

1. Wash sprouts. Cut off stems and remove any loose or discolored leaves. Cut a cross in the stem end of each. (If possible, soak sprouts in a bowl of ice water for a few hours. The cold helps to loosen the tight bulb of the sprouts.)

2. Steam sprouts in boiling salted water for 8 minutes. Drain.

3. In a large skillet, sauté shallots in butter until shallots are limp. Do not brown.

4. Add brussels sprouts and chestnuts, cover skillet, and cook about 5 minutes longer, until sprouts are just crisp-tender. Shake the pan frequently.

5. Add lemon juice and season to taste with salt and pepper. Mix in chopped dill.

6. Sprinkle top with browned bread crumbs.

▨ Sweet-and-Sour Red Cabbage

Crunchy apples and caraway seeds add sparkle to a fine vegetable that, happily for us, is available the year round. It is excellent with roast duckling, pot roast, or game.

SERVES 4 TO 6

1 medium red cabbage (about 3 pounds)
4 strips of lean bacon, diced
1 onion, finely chopped
2 tablespoons dark brown sugar
1/2 cup wine vinegar

2 tablespoons caraway seeds
salt and freshly ground pepper
1 tablespoon cornstarch (optional)
2 medium-size tart apples (preferably Granny Smith), peeled, cored, and diced

1. Remove tough outer leaves of cabbage and core. Cut into quarters. Shred the cabbage medium fine. Wash in colander under running water, drain, and set aside.

2. In a large kettle or Dutch oven, sauté diced bacon until the fat is rendered and the bacon bits are crisp.

3. Add chopped onion and sauté, stirring, until limp.

4. Add cabbage and toss well.

5. Mix together brown sugar and vinegar, and stir into cabbage. Mix in caraway seeds and season with salt and pepper.

6. Cover pot and bring to a boil. Reduce heat and simmer over lowest possible heat or an asbestos pad until cabbage is tender, 50 to 60 minutes.

7. Taste cabbage. It should be sweet-sour. If needed, adjust the taste with more sugar or vinegar, or both, 1 tablespoon at a time.

8. When the cabbage is tender and if there is too much liquid, dissolve 1 tablespoon cornstarch in a little cold water and stir into cabbage to thicken sauce.

9. Before serving, add diced apples to cabbage, toss thoroughly, and heat for 1 minute until apples are warmed. Do not cook apples.

▨ Glazed Deviled Carrots

Shiny with glaze, piquant in flavor, these carrot sticks are a fine accompaniment for a poultry or calves' liver main course.

SERVES 6

8 or 9 large carrots (about
  1½ pounds)
¼ pound (1 stick) butter
4 tablespoons light brown sugar
salt and white pepper to taste

½ to 1 teaspoon Tabasco sauce
½ teaspoon dry mustard
¼ cup dry vermouth
chopped fresh parsley or dill

1. Scrape carrots and cut into shoestrings, 3 to 4 inches long. Place in cold water.

2. In a 12-inch skillet with a cover, melt butter over moderate heat, being careful not to burn or brown it. Add brown sugar, salt, pepper, Tabasco sauce, dry mustard, and vermouth. Mix well and heat through.

3. Drain carrots quickly, leaving whatever moisture adheres to carrot pieces, and toss in butter mixture, stirring to coat evenly. Cover pan and simmer for 12 to 15 minutes, or until crisp-tender. Remove cover for the last 5 minutes of cooking to reduce sauce and to glaze carrot sticks. Sprinkle with chopped parsley or dill.

▨ Carrot Ring

A substantial crusty carrot ring that can serve as both a vegetable and a starch. For a colorful presentation, fill the center of the ring with green peas, or steamed snow peas, broccoli flowerets, a combination of snowy cauliflowerets and peas, or steamed zucchini cut in julienne strips.

SERVES 6 TO 8

1 cup solid shortening (Crisco, Spry)
1/2 cup dark brown sugar
1 large egg
2 cups coarsely grated raw carrot,
  tightly packed
1 1/2 cups all-purpose flour

1/2 teaspoon baking soda
1 teaspoon baking powder
1/2 teaspoon salt
1/2 teaspoon ground ginger
2 tablespoons orange juice
parsley sprigs

1. Grease a 3-quart ring mold with oil or shortening. Set aside.
2. In a large bowl, cream shortening and sugar until light and fluffy.
3. Beat in egg and shredded carrots, and mix well.
4. Sift together flour, baking soda, and baking powder. Add to carrot mixture with salt, ground ginger, and orange juice. Blend well and scrape into the prepared ring mold.
5. Cover mold with plastic wrap and refrigerate for 6 to 8 hours.
6. Before baking, remove from refrigerator and let stand at room temperature for 30 minutes.
7. Preheat oven to 350°. Bake carrot ring for 1 hour and 10 minutes.
8. Unmold from baking ring, garnish platter with parsley sprigs, and serve hot.

⊠ Baked Celery Hearts

I don't know why cooked celery isn't more widely served. It has a distinctive delicate flavor that never overpowers anything it accompanies, and it deserves better than being hacked up into bits and pieces for salads. Baked celery is perfect with fish, poultry, or roast meats.

SERVES 6

3 bunches celery
1¹/₂ cups chicken broth
¹/₃ cup freshly grated Parmesan
  cheese

¹/₂ cup fine bread crumbs
paprika
2 tablespoons butter
chopped parsley

1. Remove tough outer stalks of celery. Trim roots, but leave enough root to hold stalk together. Slice off tops and leaves, leaving celery heart about 6 inches long. Split celery hearts in two, lengthwise. Each half is a portion. Save celery you have cut off for soups, stews, and such. (If celery hearts seem very sandy, soak in cold water heavily laced with salt for 20 minutes. This will draw out any sand or sediment lurking in the stalks. Rinse well and drain.)

2. In a heavy skillet large enough to hold the celery hearts in a single layer, bring chicken broth to a boil, add celery hearts, and cover. Cook slowly until slightly tender, about 20 to 25 minutes, depending on celery. Test for doneness by piercing the center of the celery with a sharp-pointed knife. Do not overcook.

3. Preheat oven to 400°.

4. Remove celery hearts from skillet and place in a flat, buttered baking dish large enough to hold the celery in a single layer.

5. Sprinkle hearts with Parmesan cheese, bread crumbs, and paprika, and dot with butter.

6. Bake for 10 to 15 minutes, or until crumbs are nicely browned.

7. Transfer to heated platter and sprinkle with chopped parsley.

⊠ Corn Fritters

MAKES ABOUT 10 FRITTERS,
SERVING 4 OR 5

²/₃ cup cake flour (not self-rising)
¹/₃ cup stoneground yellow cornmeal
1 teaspoon salt
1 tablespoon sugar
2 large eggs, beaten

¹/₄ cup light cream or half-and-half
2 ears of corn
4 tablespoons (¹/₂ stick) butter
4 tablespoons vegetable oil
maple syrup and butter

1. Sift together cake flour, cornmeal, salt, and sugar. Set aside.
2. In a medium-size mixing bowl, combine eggs and cream and beat well.
3. Remove husks and silk from corn. With a sharp knife, cut kernels into workbowl of food processor.
4. With a few on-and-off motions, process kernels until pureed. Add to egg and cream mixture.
5. Add flour mixture and blend well.
6. In a large nonstick skillet, heat butter and oil. With a wooden spoon, place a large spoonful of batter in the skillet and flatten to about a 3-inch diameter. Continue until pan is full, and sauté in the hot fat until golden on each side, about 5 minutes per side. Keep warm in a 250° oven until all are done.
7. Serve with maple syrup and butter for topping.

⊠ Fresh Corn Pudding

Fresh corn niblets make this special.

SERVES 10 TO 12

2 tablespoons melted butter
10 ears fresh corn
6 eggs
2 cups half-and-half
¹/₂ cup all-purpose flour

salt and white pepper
2 tablespoons sugar
1 teaspoon nutmeg
4 tablespoons (¹/₂ stick) soft butter

1. Grease a round 10-inch baking dish, 2¹/₂ inches deep, with melted butter. Set aside.

2. Remove husks and silk from corn. With a sharp knife scraping upward, slice corn kernels into a bowl, reserving the cob. With the back of the knife scraping downward, scrape remaining part of the kernels and the milk from the cob into the same bowl. You should have 3½ to 4 cups of kernels.

3. Preheat oven to 350°.

4. With the steel blade of the food processor in place, put half the corn kernels into the workbowl with the eggs, half-and-half, flour, salt, pepper, and sugar. Process for 4 or 5 seconds with a few on-and-off turns until pureed. Stir in remainder of the kernels and mix well. Pureeing half the kernels and leaving the remainder whole gives the custard texture and body.

5. Pour mixture into the prepared baking dish. Sprinkle top with nutmeg and dot with soft butter.

6. Place baking dish in a pan in preheated oven. Add enough hot water to come halfway up the sides of the baking dish. Bake for 1 hour or until a knife inserted in the center comes out clean.

7. Serve from baking dish.

⊠ Eggplant Ciccarelli

My good friends Angela and Nico Passante introduced me to this fine Neopolitan dish. It can serve as an appetizer or for a light luncheon.

SERVES 6

3 small eggplants
½ cup olive oil
1 large garlic clove, crushed and minced
½ cup chopped green pepper
½ cup chopped red pepper
½ cup chopped fresh basil or 2 teaspoons dried basil
1½ cups ¼-inch bread cubes
salt and freshly ground pepper
2 tablespoons freshly grated Parmesan cheese
chopped parsley

1. Wash eggplants and cut in two horizontally. Carefully cut out the inside, leaving a shell about ¼ inch thick. Cut eggplant meat into ¼-inch cubes and set aside.

2. In a large skillet, heat half the oil. Add eggplant shells and sauté until just slightly softened, 7 or 8 minutes. Remove from pan with a slotted spoon and set aside.

3. Add to the pan the eggplant cubes and garlic. Cook and toss over moderate heat for 1 or 2 minutes. Add more oil if needed. Add green and red peppers and basil, and cook and stir until eggplant cubes are slightly softened, about 10 minutes.

4. In another skillet, heat remaining oil and sauté bread cubes until golden. Shake pan frequently to ensure even toasting. Remove with a slotted spoon and add to the eggplant cubes, mixing well.

5. Season with salt and pepper.

6. Fill shells with eggplant mixture and place in a baking dish. Sprinkle tops with Parmesan cheese and bake in a 350° oven for 20 to 25 minutes, or until heated through. Sprinkle with chopped parsley. Serve hot or warm.

▨ Gray Foy's Mixed Greens

Gray Foy's identification with this recipe for mixed greens comes from its being one of his favorite foods, and one that was equally popular in my mother's household. A talented artist, Gray was born in Texas and grew up in California, none of which explains his passion for this dish. He is a marvelous cook and a connoisseur of good food, and I owe him profound thanks for his inspiration and support in my producing this book.

SERVES 8 TO 12

7 pounds mixed greens (they may include collards, kale, or turnip greens)

3/4-pound slab of lean bacon, cut into 1/4-inch cubes

1 cup finely chopped onions

1/2 cup finely chopped celery

1 green pepper, cored, seeded, veins removed, and finely chopped (about 3/4 cup)

2 ham hocks, about 3/4 pound each

salt and freshly ground pepper

2 tablespoons red wine vinegar

1 or 2 dried red hot peppers, broken into pieces

2 cups water

1. Pick over greens to remove any tough stems and veins. Wash and drain thoroughly. Use only tender leaves, cutting or breaking them into 2-inch pieces. (You will have about 20 quarts, but they collapse on cooking.)

2. Put bacon in a very large, heavy kettle and cook, stirring, until rendered of fat and browned. Add onions, celery, and green pepper. Cook for about 5 minutes, stirring constantly.

3. Add greens, stirring. Cover kettle tightly and cook, stirring often, until greens are wilted. Add ham hocks, salt, pepper, vinegar, and dried pepper. Cover and cook about 15 minutes.

4. Add the water, cover, and simmer slowly for 1½ hours.

▨ Fried Okra

Okra is a popular ingredient in southern cooking, but for some reason it never achieved top billing in our household until Granny Dameron came up with the notion of frying it, which turned it into a family favorite.

Okra is at its peak from late summer through November, but the frozen is available all year. Young, fresh, tender, clean pods of small to medium size — 2 to 4 inches long — are generally of good quality.

SERVES 6

1½ pounds fresh okra or 2 10-ounce
  packages frozen okra, defrosted
2 eggs, lightly beaten
1 onion, finely chopped
¼ cup chopped fresh parsley
salt and freshly ground pepper
1 cup yellow cornmeal
safflower oil

1. Wash okra and trim off stem ends. Slice into ½-inch rounds.

2. In a shallow bowl, beat eggs and add onion, parsley, salt, and pepper, and mix well.

3. Spread a layer of cornmeal on a square of wax paper.

4. Dip okra slices into egg mixture, draining off excess, and roll in cornmeal. Add more cornmeal as needed.

5. Film bottom of large skillet with ¼ inch safflower oil, and heat.

6. Sauté okra slices, turning frequently, until tender and golden brown on each side, about 10 minutes.

7. Transfer to heated serving platter.

⊠ Baked Puree of Rutabagas

Rutabagas, also called yellow turnips (although they are a different species from turnips), rate more attention than they generally receive. They are a robust and delicious fall and winter vegetable with, most often, yellow or orange flesh, like that of the sweet potato. In Europe they are known as Swedish turnips or "Swedes." The long, slow cooking brings about a subtle and pleasing change in taste. Serve with pot roast, roast pork, or roast or broiled poultry.

SERVES 5 TO 6

2 to 3 pounds rutabagas
3 medium-size potatoes
2 tablespoons cream

2 tablespoons butter
pinch of sugar
salt and white pepper

TOPPING
½ cup fine dry bread crumbs
2 tablespoons melted butter

1. Peel rutabagas and potatoes. Cut into ½-inch slices.
2. Place in a saucepan with salted water to cover. Bring to a boil, cover pan, and boil slowly for about 30 minutes, or until tender.
3. Preheat oven to 300°. Butter a 2-quart casserole and set aside.
4. Drain vegetables thoroughly and puree them, using a vegetable mill, processor, potato masher, or ricer.
5. Beat in cream and butter. Season to taste with sugar, salt, and pepper.
6. Scrape into buttered casserole. Sprinkle top with bread crumbs and melted butter. Bake for 2 hours in slow oven.

▧ Skillet Spinach

A cross between stir-fried and steamed. The chicken broth in which the spinach cooks adds a special flavor and mellowness to the greens.

SERVES 3

1 pound tender young spinach
1/2 cup chicken broth
2 tablespoons butter

salt and freshly ground pepper
sprinkling of nutmeg

1. Pick over spinach, discarding any tired leaves and tough stems. Wash thoroughly. Washing spinach in a sinkful of lightly salted lukewarm water will remove sand more effectively than cold water. Spinach that is especially sandy should be washed in two or more changes of water. Repeat until no grit remains at bottom of sink. Drain spinach, leaving whatever water clings to the leaves.

2. In a large skillet with a lid, place chicken broth, butter, salt, and pepper, and bring to a boil.

3. Add spinach, and toss quickly and thoroughly. If the amount of spinach seems a bit much for the skillet, have faith. It will collapse shortly. Cover skillet and cook for 5 minutes, or until spinach is tender.

4. Remove spinach, drain well, sprinkle with nutmeg, mix, and serve at once.

▧ Scalloped Yellow Squash

Although classified as summer squash, yellow squash is generally available all year round. This dish can be assembled ahead of time and baked when needed.

SERVES 6 TO 8

2 1/2 to 3 pounds yellow squash (5 or
   more, depending on size)
4 tablespoons (1/2 stick) butter
2 medium onions, thinly sliced

salt and freshly ground pepper
1/4 cup grated Parmesan cheese
2/3 cup fine bread crumbs .

1. Preheat oven to 325°. Butter a deep 10- or 12-inch pie plate that can be used for serving.

2. Scrub squash and slice into ¼-inch rounds, unpeeled.

3. In a large saucepan, blanch squash in 2 quarts of boiling water and 2 tablespoons of salt for 3 minutes.

4. Drain well in a colander and spread slices over paper towels. Pat dry. Squash is a watery vegetable and does not need extra moisture.

5. In a skillet, melt 2 tablespoons butter and sauté onions until limp and transparent. Do not allow to brown.

6. Place a layer of squash slices over bottom of baking dish, slightly overlapping in concentric circles. Sprinkle lightly with salt and pepper and cover with half the onions. Continue until all is used, ending with a layer of squash. (There will be about 3 layers of squash.)

7. Sprinkle Parmesan cheese over top and cover with bread crumbs. Dot with the remaining 2 tablespoons of butter.

8. Bake for 1 hour.

▨ Broiled Tomatoes with Cheese Topping

Good with broiled meats or fish.

SERVES 4 TO 6

3 large tomatoes	*¼ cup chopped fresh parsley*
6 tablespoons mayonnaise	*2 tablespoons grated Parmesan cheese*
2 tablespoons grated onion	*white pepper*

1. Preheat broiler to medium heat.

2. Wash and dry tomatoes. Cut away stem section. Divide the tomatoes in half horizontally.

3. In a small bowl, mix together mayonnaise, onion, parsley, Parmesan cheese, and pepper.

4. Using a dessert spoon, mound mayonnaise mixture over the top of each tomato half.

5. Arrange on a baking sheet and place under the broiler at least 3 inches from the source of heat.

6. Broil for 3 to 5 minutes, or until tops are puffy and brown. (*Caution:* You must watch the tomatoes carefully to avoid burning, which can occur quickly. Keep an eye on them and don't leave them while they are under the broiler.)

⊠ Fried Tomatoes

Not only is this an agreeable side dish, but it can also make an attractive main luncheon course when served with a cheese sauce and strips of crisp, grilled bacon. It can also be prepared with firm red tomatoes, but opt for the green ones if you can get them.

SERVES 6 TO 8

4 large green tomatoes
2 eggs, beaten
1/4 cup chopped fresh parsley
1/4 cup finely chopped onions

salt and freshly ground pepper
1 cup fine dry bread crumbs
safflower oil

1. Wash and dry tomatoes. Slice away the flat stem end. Cut each tomato horizontally into about 4 thick slices.

2. In a shallow bowl, combine beaten eggs, parsley, onions, salt, and pepper.

3. Spread a layer of bread crumbs on a square of wax paper.

4. Dip both sides of tomato slices first into egg mixture — allowing the excess to drain off — and then into bread crumbs. Add more crumbs as needed.

5. Line a cookie sheet with wax paper and arrange slices in a single layer. Refrigerate for 30 minutes.

6. Film the bottom of a large skillet with oil, about 3 to 4 tablespoons. Heat oil over medium heat.

7. Sauté tomatoes on both sides until golden, turning them gently, about 2 to 3 minutes per side.

8. Place on paper towels to drain as they are done. Keep warm until all are fried. Add more oil as needed. Serve on a heated platter.

▨ Zucchini and Tomatoes

Visually pleasing, simple to prepare, and elegant enough for a formal dinner.

3 medium-size zucchini
3 medium-size tomatoes, firm
3 tablespoons butter
1 onion, finely chopped
salt and freshly ground pepper

½ cup bread crumbs
¼ cup freshly grated Parmesan
  cheese
2 tablespoons minced parsley

1. Preheat oven to 400°. Butter a 10-inch round glass or porcelain pie plate and set aside.

2. Scrub zucchini and trim the ends. Cut into ¼-inch rounds. Blanch in boiling water for 2 minutes. Drain and dry on paper towels.

3. Plunge tomatoes into boiling water for ½ minute and peel. Slice thinly and set aside.

4. In a small skillet, heat 1 tablespoon butter and sauté chopped onion until limp.

5. Alternate slices of zucchini and tomato in pie plate, arranging them in concentric circles and overlapping the slices.

6. Spread cooked onions over vegetable slices and sprinkle lightly with salt and pepper.

7. Mix together the bread crumbs and grated cheese, and sprinkle over all.

8. Dot top with remaining 2 tablespoons of butter and bake for 10 minutes, or until top is golden.

9. Sprinkle with chopped parsley and serve at once.

▒ Granny Dameron's Black-eyed Peas

Many of the traditions that flourished in my parents' home can be directly traced to Granny Dameron. New Year's Day dinner, for example. Featured always was a bowl of black-eyed peas. I can still hear her elegant, British-accented, southern drawl. "You must eat black-eyed peas on New Year's," she said. "Peas for the silver, a dab of pumpkin for the gold, and a helping of collard greens for the greenbacks." The peas were a double-edged talisman because in addition to the silver, they were guaranteed to bring a shower of good fortune in all departments throughout the coming year. I still find it impossible to plan a New Year's Day dinner without Granny Dameron's black-eyed peas, for even if they do not immediately change the course of your life for the better, they are a tasty dish.

SERVES 8 OR MORE

1 pound dried black-eyed peas
¹/₄-pound slab of lean bacon, cut into
*   ¹/₄-inch cubes (about 1 cup)*
¹/₂ cup finely chopped green or red
*   pepper*
¹/₄ cup finely chopped celery

¹/₄ cup finely chopped onion
2 teaspoons red wine vinegar
2 cups chicken broth
salt and freshly ground pepper
1 dried red pepper, crumbled
3 to 3¹/₂ cups water

1. Rinse peas and drain well.

2. Put bacon in a heavy kettle, and cook, stirring, until rendered of fat and browned. Add chopped peppers, celery, and onion, and cook, stirring, until wilted.

3. Add peas, vinegar, broth, salt, ground pepper, and dried pepper. Bring to a boil. Cover closely, reduce heat, and simmer 50 minutes.

4. Add 3 cups of water and return to a boil. Simmer over low heat about 1 hour, stirring occasionally from the bottom. Check peas and add more water if necessary. It is difficult to be specific about cooking time — peas vary in freshness and some need more time than others. They should be tender, but not mushy. Taste for doneness; they will take from about 2 to 2¹/₂ hours total cooking time.

⊠ Pan-fried Shredded Potatoes

It was on one of my early trips through Switzerland that I was first served this potato dish. It evoked memories of one my mother used to make in her trusty black iron skillet. In Switzerland it is called *Rösti;* my mother identified it by the above title. This is her version.

SERVES 4 TO 6

*2 to 2¹/₂ pounds Idaho baking
    potatoes
1 onion, grated
2 tablespoons oil*

*2 tablespoons butter
salt and freshly ground pepper
chopped fresh parsley*

1. Peel potatoes, place them in a saucepan, and cover with boiling salted water. Boil for 9 to 10 minutes. Drain thoroughly and allow the potatoes to cool. (This may be done a day in advance and the potatoes refrigerated.)

2. Shred cooled potatoes, using the coarse side of the grater, such as the one used for cabbage. Refrigerate until ready to use. (Potatoes are less likely to stick to the bottom of the pan when chilled.)

3. Mix grated onion lightly through potatoes.

4. Heat oil and butter in a 10- to 12-inch skillet (a black iron one, if you have it) over moderate heat. Add shredded potatoes and sprinkle with salt and pepper. Press potatoes gently around the sides.

5. Cook until the bottom is crusty and brown, 12 to 15 minutes. Make sure potatoes are not sticking to the bottom of the pan. Add a bit of oil if needed.

6. Place a large plate over the pan, invert the pan, and slide potatoes back into it, adding a little oil if needed. Continue cooking until underside is crusty and brown, 12 to 15 minutes longer. Sprinkle lightly with salt and pepper.

7. Slide potato cake gently out of the pan onto a round heated serving dish. Sprinkle with chopped parsley.

8. Cut into pie-shaped wedges to serve.

⊠ Parmesan Potato Gratin

SERVES 6 TO 8

2 pounds white potatoes
2 large onions
2½ cups milk

salt and freshly ground pepper
⅔ cup mayonnaise
½ cup grated Parmesan cheese

1. Preheat oven to 350°. Lightly butter a 13- or 14-inch shallow baking dish. Set aside.

2. Peel potatoes and slice thinly into a bowl of cold water. Keep them covered by 1 inch of cold water. Change the water if it becomes cloudy from the starch.

3. Peel onions and slice thinly.

4. In a large saucepan, combine potatoes and onions. Add milk and cook over moderate heat, stirring constantly to avoid having milk boil over or potatoes stick. Cook until potatoes are tender, 10 to 12 minutes.

5. Remove potatoes and onions with a slotted spoon and transfer to the baking dish. Sprinkle lightly with salt and pepper.

6. To the milk remaining in the pot, add mayonnaise and Parmesan cheese. Cook and stir for 10 minutes, until the sauce is thickened and smooth. Taste for seasoning, but chances are the Parmesan cheese will make additional salt unnecessary.

7. Pour sauce over potatoes.

8. Place in oven and bake for 40 to 45 minutes, or until top is puffy and brown. Serve hot in baking dish.

⊠ Baked Yam Casserole

A festive addition to a winter holiday dinner.

SERVES 6

2 pounds (about 6 medium) sweet po-
    tatoes, cooked and peeled
2 tablespoons melted butter
4 tablespoons light brown sugar,
    firmly packed

grated rind of 1 orange
3 to 4 tablespoons cognac
salt

3 slices white bread, crusts removed,
*   cut into ¹/₄-inch cubes*
2 tablespoons light brown sugar

1 teaspoon cinnamon
2 tablespoons melted butter

1. Preheat oven to 325°. Grease a 2-quart casserole.

2. Whip together sweet potatoes, butter, sugar, grated orange rind, and cognac until light and fluffy. Add salt to taste.

3. Scrape into greased casserole.

4. In a small bowl, toss bread cubes, sugar, and cinnamon until well combined.

5. Cover sweet potatoes with bread cube topping. Pour melted butter over all.

6. Bake for 1 hour.

⊠ Festive Rice

SERVES 6

1¹/₂ cups converted raw rice
3¹/₂ cups boiling salted water
¹/₄ cup vegetable oil
¹/₂ cup chopped green peppers

¹/₂ cup chopped sweet red peppers
¹/₂ cup chopped celery
salt and freshly ground white pepper

1. Cook rice in boiling salted water, covered, for 17 minutes. Remove from heat and let rest until all water is absorbed. Fluff with a fork.

2. In a medium skillet, heat oil. Add green and red peppers and celery, and sauté for 2 or 3 minutes. Remove from heat and set aside.

3. Oil a 1¹/₂-quart ring mold or soufflé dish.

4. Mix sautéed vegetables with cooked rice, distributing them evenly. Add salt and pepper to taste. Mound into the ring mold or soufflé dish and cover with wax paper. Place over a pot of hot water until serving time.

5. Unmold onto a round serving platter.

Camp Meeting

⊠ The annual Camp Meeting was held on the last Sunday in August in the part of North Carolina where I grew up. At this time each year, members of the Presbyterian, Baptist, and African Methodist Episcopal Zion churches came together for a revival meeting. There was a good deal of praying and singing, a fair amount of chatting and gossiping, and from the pulpit a flood of sermonizing, expounding, and declaiming. But for a small boy like me, it was the prospect of wonderful things to eat that made the Camp Meeting a red-letter day. Huge laundry baskets became picnic hampers for the occasion.

People came from far and near to participate. They came by car and on foot, the women in pastel prints with floppy straw hats suitable for a garden party and the men in their best Sunday go-to-meetin' clothes with stiff-brimmed grosgrain-banded straw hats known as boaters. It was an era of sartorial innocence, long before jeans, T-shirts, open-necked sports shirts, and polyester wash-and-wear revolutionized the fashion scene.

The all-day meeting was held in Tucker's Grove, a large grassy expanse of park and picnic grounds graced by shade trees and dotted with benches and tables. The services were held in a huge tent erected specifically for the meeting. The tent was without electricity, and the length of the meeting was limited by nature's supply of daylight.

Outside the tent, you would find groups of children attending special services arranged for them so that they would not be lost in a sea of bigger bodies brushing by. You could never miss Miss Faye, for she was always surrounded by a circle of little ones, held spellbound by the drama of her Bible stories that she illustrated with the help of a flannel board to which she attached appropriate cut-outs of biblical heroes and villains. Jonah and the Whale and Noah's Ark were two favorites.

Inside the big tent, a succession of preachers representing the different denominations took their turns on the pulpit. Some of them were electrifying and refreshing, but others were so boring and long-winded that they lulled their captive assemblage into a near coma. A lovely hundred-voice choir composed of youngsters, teen-agers, and adults filled the air with melody and harmony.

As for me, I squirmed through most of the services nourished by the knowledge that something quite wonderful was in wait. At about two o'clock in the afternoon, I would see some of the women begin to sidle out quietly, hoping not to attract attention. Granny Dameron, trim and erect in her usual black dress with the white apron and white lace collar, her head crowned with a stiff black straw hat perked up by two tall black feathers that jutted skyward into a V like a bird in flight (we called it her "crow hat"), was among the first to leave. She was followed shortly afterward by Miss Elmina, a thin little lady with gray hair parted in the middle and drawn back into a sedate knot. Then came Miss Dulcina. She looked, I thought, like an Egyptian queen, with her delicate aquiline features and satiny mahogany-colored skin. A bit later Miss Oresta made her exit. I considered Miss Oresta the stylish member of Granny Dameron's entourage because she never appeared in public without her gloves, hat, and pocketbook. All this activity was my signal and reassurance that serious business was going on outside the tent.

Soon the services came to a temporary halt. The congregants thronged outside, and it became quickly apparent that praying and singing hymns whet the appetite. Picnic tables were heaped with food. Each family had brought its own hamper, but people visited friends and kinfolk at other tables where they sampled, gorged, and exchanged recipes.

Granny Dameron's menu generally included baked ham, fried chicken, tea sandwiches, cheese straws, yeast rolls, coconut cake, sweet potato pie, watermelon pickles, a salad of pickled beets and hard-boiled eggs, a huge assortment of cookies, and quantities of iced tea sparked with fresh mint and orange juice.

Nightfall brought the Camp Meeting to an end. It was always an unforgettable day, marked by a spirit of reverence, of profound friendship, and of loving and sharing.

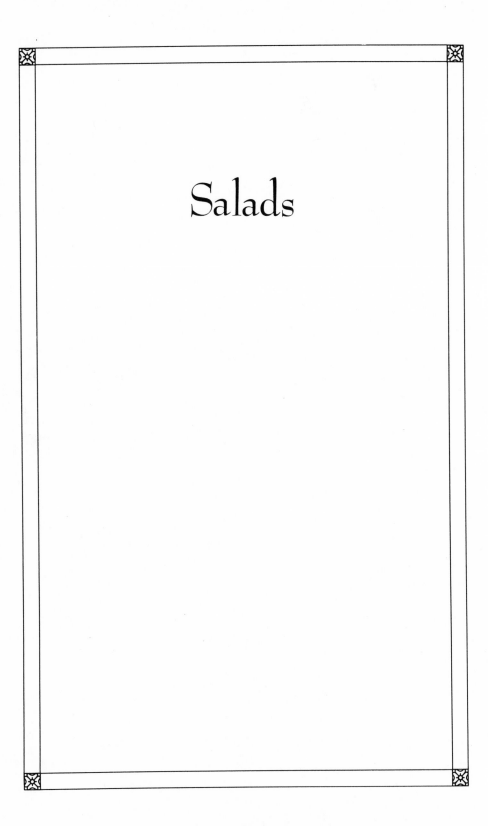

Salads

⊠ Vinaigrette Dressing

MAKES ABOUT 2½ CUPS

1 cup safflower or other good vegetable oil
½ cup sherry wine vinegar
½ cup water

3 tablespoons Dijon mustard
½ cup finely chopped red onion
1 tablespoon sugar
salt and freshly ground pepper

1. Place all ingredients in a jar with a tight-fitted lid.
2. Shake like a martini, and keep refrigerated.

⊠ Pickled Beet and Egg Salad

Colorful and piquant.

SERVES 6 TO 8

10 to 12 medium-size beets
1 teaspoon salt
1½ cups wine vinegar
3 tablespoons honey
4 cloves

5 hard-cooked eggs, peeled and left
   whole
red-tipped lettuce
minced fresh parsley

1. Wash beets gently, leaving root ends and about 2 inches of stem attached.
2. Cook in boiling water to cover. Cover pot tightly and cook for 25 to 35 minutes, or until tender to the touch of a finger. Pricking beets to test for doneness will cause beets to bleed and lose their rosy color.
3. Remove beets from pot and slip off skins when cool enough to handle. Slice beets ¼ inch thick and place in large bowl.
4. Combine salt, vinegar, honey, and cloves in a small saucepan and bring to a boil. Pour over beets. When completely cool, add hard-cooked eggs and refrigerate, covered, for at least 24 hours before serving.
5. To serve, cut eggs in quarters. Line a platter with red-tipped lettuce and arrange slices of beets alternating with the egg segments. Sprinkle lightly with minced fresh parsley.

⊠ Cauliflower Salad ✱✱

Good with cold baked ham or cold meats.

SERVES 6

1 large head cauliflower
1/2 cup finely chopped celery
2 hard-cooked eggs, coarsely chopped
1/4 cup chopped shallots
1/4 cup pimientos, drained and
   chopped
1/3 cup mayonnaise

1 teaspoon lemon juice
1 teaspoon Dijon mustard
1 tablespoon sour cream
salt and freshly ground pepper
lettuce
2 tomatoes, peeled and cut into
   wedges

1. Break cauliflower into flowerets and rinse well.
2. Bring four cups of salted water to a boil. Add cauliflowerets and let come to a boil. Reduce heat, cover, and simmer for 10 to 12 minutes, until crisp-tender. Do not overcook.
3. Drain, transfer to a bowl, and cool completely.
4. Add celery, eggs, shallots, and pimientos to cauliflower and toss.
5. In a small bowl, blend mayonnaise, lemon juice, mustard, and sour cream. Toss with cauliflower.
6. Season to taste with salt and pepper.
7. Serve on a bed of lettuce and garnish with tomato wedges.

⊠ Chicken Salad

A chicken salad that is light, delicious, and a bit different from the usual. Lovely for a picnic or as an additional offering on a buffet table.

SERVES 8

4 cups chicken broth, fresh or canned
2 large onions, quartered
bouquet garni*
6- to 7-pound capon, cleaned
salt and freshly ground pepper
1 medium-size green bell pepper,
    roasted
1 medium-size red bell pepper, roasted

1 large carrot
1 dill pickle
1/4 cup fresh lemon juice
salt and freshly ground pepper
1/2 cup good-quality virgin olive oil
lettuce leaves and lemon slices
2 tablespoons small capers (optional)

1. In a large kettle or Dutch oven, place chicken broth, onions, *bouquet garni,* and chicken. Slowly bring to a boil. Reduce heat, partially cover, and simmer slowly for 50 to 55 minutes, skimming as needed. Season with salt and pepper to taste. Turn off heat and let bird cool in the broth, breast side down.

2. To roast peppers, place washed and dried peppers on a baking sheet or foil broiling pan under preheated broiler. Broil until charred and softened, turning until all surfaces are darkened. Transfer to a brown paper bag and close securely so that peppers will steam. As soon as they are cool enough to handle, 10 or 15 minutes, remove from bag, cut into halves vertically, and scrape the blackened skin away under running water. Trim away cores, seeds, and membranes, and cut peppers into 1/4-inch julienne strips. Refrigerate until needed.

3. When the bird is cool, remove from broth. Discard skin and strip off meat from bone. (Strain broth and refrigerate or freeze for another use.)

4. Cut chicken meat into julienne strips, about 2 inches long and 1/2 inch wide. Place in a large glass or ceramic bowl, cover, and refrigerate.

5. Scrape carrot and cut into julienne strips. Cut dill pickle into julienne strips. Set aside.

6. Mix lemon juice with salt and pepper. Slowly beat in olive oil.

7. Just before serving, combine chicken and julienne vegetables. Toss with the dressing.

8. Transfer to a serving platter lined with lettuce leaves. Sprinkle salad with capers. Garnish with lemon slices.

Bouquet garni is a combination of herbs and spices, tied together in a square of cheesecloth fastened with a string or in a stainless metal tea ball. Basic herbs for a *bouquet garni* are parsley, thyme, and bay leaf to which may be added a variety of other herbs, such as chervil, basil, marjoram, or savory.

▨ Chicken, Apple, and Walnut Salad

3 whole chicken breasts, boned and
  skinned
¹/₄ cup sherry wine vinegar
1 teaspoon dried tarragon
¹/₄ cup salad oil
salt and freshly ground pepper
2 tablespoons fresh lemon juice

1 cup ice water
3 Granny Smith apples (medium size)
¹/₂ cup walnut halves
2 tablespoons butter
Boston or red-edged lettuce
vinaigrette dressing (page 145)

1. Cut chicken breasts in half.

2. In a glass or porcelain or stainless-steel bowl (not aluminum), mix vinegar, tarragon, oil, salt, and pepper. Marinate chicken for 30 minutes.

3. In another bowl, combine lemon juice and ice water.

4. Peel and core apples and slice into thin wedges. Place apple slices in lemon juice mixture and refrigerate.

5. Place chicken breasts in a skillet large enough to hold the breasts in a single layer. Add marinade and cook, covered, over moderate heat until done, about 20 minutes, turning a few times. Do not overcook; overcooking toughens chicken meat.

6. Spread walnuts in a single layer on a flat pan. Dot with butter and bake for 15 to 20 minutes in a 325° oven. Shake the pan from time to time. Watch carefully to avoid overbrowning. Remove from oven when crisp.

7. Drain chicken breasts and cut into diagonal slices. Line a serving platter with lettuce leaves, and arrange chicken slices in the center of the platter in concentric circles, slices overlapping.

8. Drain apples and pat dry. Border the circle of chicken slices with apple slices. Sprinkle lightly with vinaigrette dressing and scatter walnuts over all. Pass additional vinaigrette dressing.

▨ Curried Chicken and Vegetable Salad

SERVES 6 TO 8

3 2½-pound broilers
6 cups chicken broth, fresh or canned
3 tablespoons curry powder
2 whole large onions, peeled and cut
   into quarters
salt and freshly ground pepper
1 cup cooked peas
1 cup cooked string beans, broken
   into quarters

½ cup chopped celery
½ cup cooked chopped carrots
¼ cup chopped shallots
½ cup (or more) mayonnaise
1 tablespoon curry powder
lettuce
condiments

1. Rinse chickens inside and out, and place in a large soup kettle with chicken broth, curry powder, onions, salt, and pepper.

2. Bring slowly to a boil. Reduce heat and simmer, partially covered, until chickens are tender, 45 to 50 minutes.

3. Remove chickens from broth and let cool. When cool enough to handle, remove meat from bones, discard skin, and cut chickens into ½-inch cubes.

4. Add vegetables to chicken and mix well.

5. Combine mayonnaise and 1 tablespoon curry powder (or more or less, according to taste), add to chicken, and mix well. Cover bowl and refrigerate for several hours.

6. Line a large platter with lettuce leaves.

7. Taste salad and add seasonings if desired. If mixture seems dry, add additional mayonnaise, but avoid coating too heavily.

8. Serve with small bowls of some of the following condiments:

diced apple marinated in
   lemon juice
raisins soaked in sherry
chopped peanuts

toasted almonds
coconut
chutney
chopped cucumber

⊠ Coleslaw

1 small head white cabbage
1 small head red cabbage
1 carrot, grated
1 teaspoon sugar
1/2 cup mayonnaise
2 tablespoons finely chopped shallots

2 tablespoons chopped fresh parsley
1 teaspoon Dijon mustard
1/4 cup sour cream
1 teaspoon celery seed
salt and freshly ground pepper

1. Cut the heads of cabbage in half, place in a bowl of cold water, and refrigerate for 1 hour. Drain well.

2. Shred cabbages finely. You should have 2 to 3 cups of each. Place in a bowl.

3. Add grated carrot and sugar, and toss.

4. In another bowl, combine mayonnaise, shallots, parsley, mustard, sour cream, and celery seed. Season with salt and pepper. Add to sliced cabbage and toss well.

5. Taste for seasoning and correct, and refrigerate until ready to serve.

⊠ Fresh Corn and Bacon Salad

SERVES 4 TO 6

6 to 8 ears of fresh corn
1/2 pound bacon
1 large green pepper, finely chopped
1 small red onion, finely chopped
1/2 cup fresh tomato, seeded and
  chopped
1 2-ounce jar chopped pimientos, well
  drained

1/3 cup chopped fresh cilantro, leaves
  only — no stems (if unavailable,
  use parsley)
vinaigrette dressing (page 145)
salt and freshly ground pepper
Boston lettuce
cherry tomatoes or sliced tomatoes

1. Remove husks and silk from corn. With a sharp knife, cut kernels into a bowl.

2. Bring 4 cups of water and a tablespoon of salt to a boil. Add corn kernels and cook for 5 minutes, covered. Run under cold water to stop the oooking. Drain well and set aside.

3. Chop bacon very fine and fry until crisp. Drain on paper towels.

4. Toss corn with green pepper, onion, tomato, pimientos, cilantro, and enough vinaigrette dressing to moisten, about ½ cup. Add salt and pepper, if desired.

5. To serve, mound corn salad on a bed of Boston lettuce and sprinkle top with crisp bacon bits. Garnish platter with cherry tomatoes or sliced tomatoes.

Note: Scooped-out tomato shells filled with corn salad make a fine salad course, or a vegetable with cold chicken or a meat or fish salad. Corn salad can also be used to stuff small zucchini shells. Cut the zucchini lengthwise and scoop out the pulp, leaving about ¼ inch of shell. Blanch the shells in boiling water for 2 minutes. Cool and fill with corn salad.

⊠ Cucumber Salad

SERVES 6

1 long seedless cucumber, or 2 large
regular cucumbers (3 to 4 cups,
sliced)
¼ cup sherry wine vinegar
salt and freshly ground pepper

1 teaspoon sugar
½ cup sour cream
¼ cup finely chopped fresh dill
Bibb or Boston lettuce
additional dill

1. Peel cucumber and slice thinly. Transfer to a bowl.

2. Pour vinegar over and toss quickly with salt, pepper, and sugar.

3. Transfer to a strainer and allow to drain thoroughly. Return to bowl.

4. Combine sour cream and dill. Toss with cucumbers.

5. Serve on lettuce leaves with more chopped dill for garnish.

⊠ Lima Bean Salad

This goes well with cold sliced lamb on a hot day.

SERVES 6 TO 8

2 10-ounce packages frozen baby
   lima beans
1/4 cup chopped fresh dill
1/4 cup chopped shallots
1/4 cup chopped parsley
1 chopped hard-cooked egg

1/4 cup mayonnaise
1/4 cup sour cream
1 tablespoon tarragon vinegar
salt and freshly ground pepper
lettuce
tomato wedges

1. Cook lima beans according to package directions. Cool under cold running water and drain well.
2. At serving time, mix in dill, shallots, parsley, and chopped egg.
3. In a small bowl, blend together the mayonnaise, sour cream, and vinegar. Toss with beans. Add salt and pepper to taste.
4. Serve on a bed of lettuce with wedges of tomatoes.

⊠ Pasta Salad with Tuna

A zesty pasta salad, a glass of your favorite wine, and a warm loaf of crusty Italian bread add up to a summer delight for lunch, supper, or a picnic in the park. Fusilli is the pasta that is twisted like a short, tight corkscrew.

SERVES 6

1 pound fusilli
1/2 cup chopped fresh tomatoes (preferably firm Italian plum tomatoes)
3 tablespoons capers, drained and
   chopped
1/4 cup chopped black olives
1/4 cup chopped fresh parsley
1/4 cup chopped pimientos, drained

1 small green pepper, chopped
   (optional)
1 small red onion, finely chopped
1/2 cup grated Parmesan cheese
2 6 1/2- to 7-ounce cans water-packed
   white meat tuna, drained
1/2 cup (or more) vinaigrette dressing
   (page 145)
salt and freshly ground pepper

1. Cook pasta according to package directions until *al dente*. Drain and run under cold water. Drain thoroughly and set aside to cool.

2. Combine all remaining ingredients with the cooked and cooled pasta. Toss with vinaigrette dressing and blend. Add salt and pepper to taste.

3. Chill for at least 30 minutes before serving.

⊠ Summer Salad

This makes an attractive presentation for a buffet or as a cold vegetable for any occasion.

SERVES 6

3 medium-size zucchini
2 medium-size yellow squash
4 carrots, scraped
1 small red onion

1 pint cherry tomatoes
1 bunch watercress
vinaigrette dressing (page 145)
chopped fresh parsley

1. Scrub zucchini and yellow squash with a vegetable brush and remove end tips.

2. Slice zucchini, yellow squash, and carrots into ¼-inch rounds, keeping each vegetable separate.

3. In a medium-size pot, bring 4 cups of water and 1 tablespoon of salt to a boil. Blanch zucchini in the boiling water for 1 or 2 minutes and scoop out with a strainer. Refresh under cold running water. Repeat with yellow squash for 2 or 3 minutes and refresh under cold water. Cook carrots only until crisp-tender and refresh under cold water.

4. Peel onion, slice thinly, and set aside.

5. Wash cherry tomatoes and remove stems.

6. Wash watercress, dry, and remove thickest part of the stems.

7. Arrange watercress along the outside rim of a serving platter. Place a row of yellow squash over the watercress; a circle of zucchini overlapping the squash a bit; a circle of carrot slices; and a mound of cherry tomatoes in the center. Scatter onion slices over the vegetables.

8. Sprinkle with vinaigrette dressing and chopped parsley. Serve chilled.

⊠ New Red Potato Salad

Red-skinned potatoes have a waxy quality that makes them a good choice for potato salad because they won't soak up the dressing or crumble when cut into cubes or slices. Since much of the potato's nutrients are stored in the layer beneath the skin, it is desirable not to peel them.

SERVES 6

2 pounds new red potatoes
1/2 cup finely chopped celery
1/3 cup finely chopped red onion
3 hard-cooked eggs, chopped
1/4 cup minced fresh parsley
1/2 cup homemade mayonnaise
  (page 161)

1 tablespoon white vinegar
1 tablespoon Dijon mustard
salt and freshly ground pepper
lettuce
cherry tomatoes

1. Scrub potatoes and cut into large chunks. Place in a saucepan and cover with salted water. Cover and bring to a boil. Reduce heat and cook until tender, about 15 minutes. Do not overcook.

2. Drain thoroughly and transfer to a bowl. Cool.

3. Add celery, onion, hard-cooked eggs, and parsley to potatoes and toss.

4. In a small bowl, combine mayonnaise, vinegar, and mustard. Add to potatoes and toss.

5. Season with salt and pepper to taste.

6. Serve in a bowl or platter on a bed of crisp lettuce and garnish with cherry tomatoes.

Note: For an attractive presentation, line a 1-quart mold with plastic wrap and pack potato salad into mold. Cover and refrigerate for several hours. Unmold on a platter, inverting the mold. Peel off plastic wrap. Garnish with parsley sprigs and radish roses.

▨ Tomato and Red Onion Salad

A harmonious contrast in textures and colors makes for a refreshing salad that can also serve as a first course. The combination of the salt and sugar — a practice initiated by my mother — does something very exciting to the flavor of the tomatoes: the sugar sweetens and the salt heightens, with a splendid result.

SERVES 5

3 large ripe beefsteak tomatoes
2 tablespoons sugar
1 tablespoon salt

1 large red onion, thinly sliced
vinaigrette dressing (page 145)
fresh basil leaves

1. Wash tomatoes and cut out the black core stem with a sharp knife.
2. Plunge tomatoes into a pot of boiling water for 1 to 2 minutes.
3. Remove from the boiling water and run under cold water.
4. Starting at the top, gently peel off the skins.
5. Slice thickly. You should get 5 substantial slices from each tomato.
6. Mix together the sugar and salt. Sprinkle over both sides of each slice.
7. Alternate slices of tomato and onion on individual plates, allowing three slices of tomato per serving.
8. Sprinkle with vinaigrette dressing and garnish salad with fresh basil leaves.

▨ Individual Tomato Aspics

The unexpected in these zesty aspics is a nugget of seasoned, textured cream cheese nestling in their centers. The aspics make a fine first course or a luncheon salad served with a cheese soufflé.

SERVES 10 TO 12

1-quart 14-ounce can V-8 juice
1 large onion, coarsely chopped
4 celery stalks, coarsely chopped
1/2 cup dry white wine
1/2 cup cold water
4 tablespoons unflavored gelatin
salt
dash of red pepper or Tabasco sauce
1/4 cup cider vinegar

1/2 pound cream cheese
1 medium onion, finely minced
1 medium green bell pepper, finely
  chopped
dash of red pepper
salt if desired
watercress and Belgian endive
vinaigrette dressing (page 145)

1. Oil 10 to 12 molds, such as large muffin tins or custard cups. Set aside.

2. In a 2-quart saucepan, combine V-8 juice with chopped onion and celery. Slowly bring to a boil, reduce heat, and simmer gently, uncovered, for 30 minutes.

3. While juice is cooking, combine wine and water in a small bowl. Sprinkle gelatin over and allow to soften.

4. Strain V-8 liquid when cooking is completed and return to pot. Discard vegetables.

5. Season liquid with salt and red pepper or Tabasco sauce to taste. Add dissolved gelatin, and stir over low heat until all the granules are dissolved and the juice is clear. Mix in vinegar.

6. Fill molds three-quarters full and refrigerate.

7. In a small bowl, mash together cream cheese, onion, and green pepper. Season to taste with red pepper and salt, and mix well. Form into small balls, about the size of a large cherry.

8. When aspics have thickened to the consistency of thick egg white, tuck a cheese ball down into the center of each mold. Chill until set.

9. Unmold on individual plates to serve. Garnish with watercress and Belgian endive, and sprinkle with vinaigrette dressing.

Sauces

◻ Béchamel Sauce

4 tablespoons (¹/₂ stick) butter
4 tablespoons flour

2 cups milk
salt and freshly ground pepper

1. Melt butter in a medium-size, heavy-bottomed saucepan.
2. Blend in the flour, stirring with a wooden spoon. Stir and cook for 2 to 3 minutes, until flour and butter bubble and foam.
3. Remove from the heat and add milk. Beat vigorously with a wire whisk.
4. Return to the heat and continue whisking until sauce is thickened and smooth, 5 to 6 minutes longer.
5. Season to taste with salt and pepper. Remove from heat, and cover closely with wax paper to prevent a skin from forming if sauce is not to be used at once.

◻ Creole Sauce

Good with broiled fish, fishcakes, rice, and pasta.

MAKES ABOUT 3 CUPS

4 tablespoons (¹/₂ stick) butter
1 medium onion, finely chopped
1 clove garlic, finely minced
2 cups chopped canned Italian
  tomatoes, drained

1 cup clam broth or fish stock
¹/₂ teaspoon dried thyme
dash of hot pepper sauce
1 tablespoon dry sherry

1. In a medium saucepan, heat butter. Add onions and garlic, and sauté, stirring, over moderate heat until onions are wilted but not brown.
2. Add all remaining ingredients except sherry and simmer slowly for 30 to 40 minutes, stirring occasionally so that sauce does not scorch.
3. Before serving, add sherry and heat through. Taste and correct seasoning.

▥ Blender Hollandaise Sauce

MAKES ABOUT ³/₄ CUP

3 egg yolks
2 tablespoons fresh lemon juice
¹/₄ teaspoon salt
white pepper

¹/₂ teaspoon Dijon mustard
¹/₂ cup (1 stick) unsalted butter,
   melted and hot

1. Place all ingredients except melted butter in a blender and blend until eggs are foamy, about 5 seconds.
2. Heat butter until it sizzles, but do not let it brown.
3. Remove the insert from the cover of the blender (leaving the cover on helps to prevent spattering) and, with the machine running, pour in the bubbling hot butter in a thin, steady stream. It will thicken quickly, in a matter of seconds. If sauce is too thick, stir in 1 to 2 tablespoons hot water. Taste and correct seasonings; you may want a dash of Tabasco or cayenne pepper.

Note: Hollandaise may be made well in advance. Rinse a thermos bottle with hot water and pour freshly made sauce into it. The hollandaise will keep warm until you are ready to use it.

▥ Tartar Sauce

MAKES ABOUT 1¹/₂ CUPS

¹/₂ cup mayonnaise (preferably home-
   made)
¹/₂ cup sour cream
2 tablespoons drained chopped capers
2 tablespoons finely chopped shallots
1 tablespoon chopped pimiento-stuffed
   olives

1 teaspoon Dijon mustard
1 tablespoon lemon juice
white pepper to taste
dash of vodka
1 hard-boiled egg yolk, forced
   through a strainer (optional)

1. Combine all ingredients and blend well.
2. Taste for seasoning and correct. Keep refrigerated.

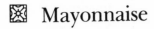 # Mayonnaise

1 whole egg	*½ teaspoon dry mustard*
2 tablespoons lemon juice	*½ teaspoon Dijon mustard*
1 teaspoon salt	*½ cup olive oil*
¼ teaspoon white pepper	*½ cup vegetable oil*

1. With the metal blade in place, put all ingredients except the oils in container of a food processor. Process until well blended and slightly thickened. Continue processing and slowly add the oil through the feed tube. As mayonnaise becomes thicker, you will notice that the sound of the machine deepens, at which point the oil may be added more quickly.

2. Taste for seasonings and correct if necessary.

3. Transfer to a covered container and refrigerate.

VARIATIONS

Substitute white wine vinegar for lemon juice.
Green Mayonnaise: Add ½ cup chopped fresh spinach or ¼ cup chopped fresh dill to egg mixture in processor.
Shallot Mayonnaise: Add ¼ cup chopped shallots to egg mixture in processor.

▨ Clarified Butter

Clarified butter will stay fresh for weeks because the casein and the whey, which are subject to bacterial change, have been removed. It has a much higher burning point than butter and thus is a good choice for delicate sautéeing in which you want to avoid browned butter.

MAKES ¾ CUP CLARIFIED BUTTER

½ pound (2 sticks) butter

1. Preheat oven to 300°. Cut butter into small pieces and place in a heatproof bowl in oven. Allow to remain until butter is melted.
2. Remove from oven. Skim off the foam (casein) and discard.
3. Let stand for a few minutes to allow milk solids to settle. Skim the clear yellow liquid off the milky residue (whey) left on the bottom and store in a covered jar in the refrigerator. The clear liquid is the clarified butter. Discard the residue.

▨ Watercress Butter

A topping for meat or fish or a bread-spread for sandwiches.

MAKES ABOUT 10 TABLESPOONS

½ bunch watercress
¼ pound (1 stick) soft butter

1. Wash watercress and pat dry. Discard coarse stems. Place in food processor with butter and process with a few on-and-off turns until combined.
2. Scrape out of processor, form into a roll, and wrap in plastic wrap. Refrigerate and use as needed.

Dessert Sauces

▧ Chocolate Sauce

MAKES ABOUT 1¼ CUPS

*8-ounce package semisweet chocolate
  morsels*
¼ cup light brown sugar

*¼ cup light cream or half-and-half,
  very hot*

Place all ingredients in workbowl of processor and process until smooth.

Note: For a more provocative flavor, add 1 tablespoon cognac or 1 tablespoon grated orange rind and 1 teaspoon Grand Marnier.

▧ Lemon Sauce

MAKES ABOUT 2½ CUPS

*2½ tablespoons cornstarch or
  arrowroot*
1 cup superfine sugar
2 tablespoons grated lemon rind

1 cup water
1 cup lemon juice
½ teaspoon salt
¼ cup (½ stick) melted butter

1. In a heavy-bottomed, nonaluminum saucepan, combine cornstarch, sugar, and lemon rind.
2. Combine water and lemon juice in a bowl.
3. Add liquid to saucepan slowly over medium heat, stirring constantly until thickened and smooth.
4. Remove from heat and stir in salt and melted butter. Serve warm.

⊠ Hard Sauce

¹/₂ cup (1 stick) butter at room
  temperature
1 cup confectioner's sugar, sifted

1 teaspoon grated lemon rind
1 teaspoon vanilla extract

1. In a small bowl, cream the butter. Gradually beat in confectioner's sugar and continue creaming the mixture until light and fluffy.
2. Mix in lemon rind and vanilla extract. Chill and serve cold.

⊠ Vanilla Cream Sauce

MAKES ABOUT 3 CUPS

4 large egg yolks
¹/₂ cup granulated sugar
1 cup milk
1 cup heavy cream

1 teaspoon vanilla extract
¹/₄ cup Grand Marnier, cognac,
  kirsch, or sweet sherry

1. In a heavy-bottomed, nonaluminum saucepan, beat egg yolks and sugar until thick and lemon-colored, using a wooden spoon or a stainless steel whisk.
2. In another saucepan, bring milk and cream just to a boil.
3. Very slowly, stir cream mixture into egg yolk mixture and mix well, making sure that sugar is dissolved.
4. Cook custard over low heat, stirring constantly, until it is thick enough to coat spoon. Keep the heat low and avoid having the custard boil or it will curdle.
5. Transfer custard to a bowl placed in a larger bowl filled with cracked ice, and stir until cooled.
6. Cover top closely with plastic wrap to prevent a skin from forming and let cool. When cool, mix in vanilla extract and liqueur or sherry. Cover with plastic wrap and refrigerate. Serve chilled.

Muffins,
Quick Breads,
and
Rolls

Muffins, Quick Breads, and Rolls

Muffins are one of the simplest of all quick breads to prepare. The ingredients need only to be mixed together briefly; no extensive beating is required. Served hot, they add substance and variety to a breakfast or simple supper.

I find it convenient to use an ice cream scoop when filling the muffin tins. The scoop gives the muffins a neat rounded shape and makes the business of filling the tins quick and easy.

▨ Banana Bran Muffins ⚘⚘⚘

These are a delicious, hearty breakfast treat, served with butter and jam, or hot out of the oven and unadorned, plus a tall glass of milk or a cup of steaming coffee or tea.

Extra batter can be refrigerated and baked as needed.

17
MAKES 12 3-INCH OR 18 2½-INCH
MUFFINS

1 cup bran
1 cup buttermilk
2 eggs, lightly beaten
½ cup molasses
1 cup mashed ripe bananas (about 2)
½ cup raisins or dried currants

¼ cup wheat germ
1¼ cups whole wheat flour
½ teaspoon salt
2 teaspoons baking powder
1 teaspoon baking soda

too hot!

1. Preheat oven to 425°. Butter the muffin pan generously and place in oven to heat. *400°*

2. Soak bran in buttermilk for 10 minutes.

3. Add beaten eggs, molasses, bananas, raisins, and wheat germ, and mix.

4. Sift the flour, salt, baking powder, and baking soda. Add to bran mixture and stir just enough to dampen.

5. Using a medium-size ice cream scoop, place scoops of batter into the greased muffin tins.

6. Place in preheated oven and bake for 15 minutes.

7. Let muffins rest a few minutes before removing from the pan. Serve warm.

⊠ Blueberry Muffins

A harbinger of summer, blueberries are available in most areas from May through September, reaching their peak in July. Blueberry muffins, slathered with whipped butter, are a fine breakfast treat or a teatime snack.

MAKES 12 3-INCH MUFFINS

1 cup blueberries
2 cups all-purpose flour
1/4 cup sugar
2 teaspoons baking powder
1/2 teaspoon baking soda

1/2 teaspoon salt
2 large eggs, lightly beaten
1/2 cup sour cream
1 teaspoon vanilla extract

TOPPING
3 tablespoons melted butter
2 tablespoons sugar
1/2 teaspoon cinnamon

1. Rinse blueberries, drain well, and spread out on paper towels to dry.

2. Preheat oven to 400°. Grease muffin tin and place in oven to heat.

3. Sift all dry ingredients into a bowl. Reserve a few tablespoons of flour to sprinkle over blueberries to keep them from sinking in the batter.

4. In a separate bowl, combine beaten eggs, sour cream, and vanilla, and blend well.

5. Add sour cream mixture to dry ingredients, stirring only enough to dampen flour. The batter need not be smooth.

6. Sprinkle the reserved flour over blueberries and gently fold them into batter.

7. With a medium-size ice cream scoop, scoop batter into muffin tins, filling each cup about two-thirds full.

8. Bake for about 20 minutes, or until nicely brown.

9. Remove from oven, brush the tops of each muffin with melted butter, and sprinkle with sugar and cinnamon mixed together. Let muffins rest for 1 or 2 minutes before removing from baking pan.

▨ Buttermilk Biscuits

My mother did not consider a meal in her home complete without a platter of her golden, crusty buttermilk biscuits. She embellished leftover dough with sugar, raisins, and honey, producing a confection that we children descriptively labeled "stickies." Delicious.

MAKES 12 TO 14 BISCUITS

2 cups all-purpose flour
1½ teaspoons sugar
½ teaspoon salt
3 teaspoons baking powder

½ teaspoon baking soda
¼ pound (1 stick) butter
¼ cup buttermilk
1 egg, lightly beaten

1. Preheat oven to 450°. Grease a large baking sheet.
2. Sift all dry ingredients together in a mixing bowl.
3. Cut in butter and work in with pastry blender or your fingertips until mixture resembles coarse meal.
4. In a separate bowl, combine buttermilk and egg.
5. Add to flour mixture and stir until a soft dough forms.
6. Turn dough out onto a lightly floured surface and knead for a minute or so to thoroughly blend ingredients.
7. Roll out or pat dough to a thickness of ½ inch. Cut into rounds with a 2-inch cookie cutter. Gather up the remaining dough, pat to the required thickness, and cut rounds until all dough is used.
8. Place on a baking sheet, leaving 1 inch of space between, and bake for 12 to 15 minutes, until golden brown. (These biscuits are best when served hot, directly from the oven.)

VARIATIONS

Cheese Biscuits: Add 1 cup grated sharp cheddar cheese and a pinch of cayenne pepper to dry ingredients.
"Stickies": Roll out leftover dough into a rectangle. Spread top with soft butter. Mix a little cinnamon and light brown sugar together and sprinkle over dough. Spread some raisins over all and pat them down into dough. Roll like a jelly roll. Cut into 1-inch slices and place them in a small greased baking dish, touching each other. Bake in a 350° oven for 20 to 25 minutes, or until golden. Five minutes before they are done, paint the tops with a mixture of melted butter and honey and return to oven.

▨ Bacon Bread

Among my many childhood food memories is my grandmother's crackling bread, a delicious concoction made from pork skin renderings. In my version, I introduce crisp bacon for flavor and sour cream for lightness and texture. This is a quick bread that is indeed quick and makes a lovely gift.

MAKES 1 LOAF

2 cups all-purpose flour
3 teaspoons baking powder
pinch of salt (optional)
6 strips of bacon

2 eggs
²/₃ cup sour cream
3 tablespoons melted butter

1. Preheat oven to 350°. Grease a 5- by 8-inch bread pan, line with wax paper, and grease paper. Set aside.
2. Sift flour, baking powder, and salt. (Salt may be omitted, since bacon is generally a bit salty.)
3. Fry bacon until very crisp. Place on paper towels to drain. Crumble into small pieces.
4. In a small bowl, mix eggs, sour cream, and melted butter.
5. Stir sour cream mixture into dry ingredients and blend.
6. Fold bacon pieces into batter.
7. Scrape into prepared pan and even top. Bake for 50 to 55 minutes, or until top is nicely browned and a cake tester comes out dry.
8. Cool on rack. When cool, invert pan and remove paper. This bread may be served warm or at room temperature.

▧ Super Cornbread

The basic recipe for cornbread, corn muffins, and corn sticks.

SERVES 6 OR MORE

6 tablespoons butter-flavored vegeta-
ble shortening (such as butter-
flavored Crisco)
1 cup cake flour (not self-rising)
1 cup yellow stoneground cornmeal
1 teaspoon sugar

1 teaspoon salt
2½ teaspoons baking powder
1 teaspoon baking soda
8-ounce can cream-style corn
2 large eggs, slightly beaten
1 cup sour cream

1. Preheat oven to 400°. Grease a 9- by 12-inch baking dish, 1½ to 2 inches deep, with 2 tablespoons of the shortening. Place in the heated oven for 5 minutes before filling.

2. Sift together flour, cornmeal, sugar, salt, baking powder, and baking soda. Place in a medium-size bowl.

3. Melt the remaining 4 tablespoons of shortening and keep warm.

4. In a small bowl, blend together the corn, eggs, and cup of sour cream. Pour over dry ingredients and mix well.

5. Mix in the heated shortening. Pour batter into baking dish and bake for 30 to 35 minutes, until top is golden brown.

VARIATION

Cornmeal Muffins or Corn Sticks: Grease 12 large muffin tins or corn stick pans generously with shortening. Place in heated oven for 5 minutes before filling. Fill heated tins two-thirds full. Bake 20 to 30 minutes or until nicely browned and baked through.

⊠ Pumpkin Bread

Uniquely American, pumpkins grew in South and Central America and Mexico long before the arrival of the first Europeans. The pumpkin has the added distinction of being a vegetable that has successfully spilled over into the dessert area as a pie filling or in custards, a not easily duplicated feat in the vegetable world.

My mother's garden in North Carolina abounded with pumpkins, and every fall season would find her back porch studded with stacks of them in a variety of sizes. She was never at a loss for what to do about all this hard-shelled orange bounty. A steady stream of pumpkin pies, ice cream, custards, puddings, muffins, and bread found its way to our table. Sometimes she served the pumpkin unadorned as a vegetable side dish or in a beef stew in place of potatoes.

One of my favorites is the pumpkin bread that follows. It is more cake than bread.

MAKES 1 9- BY 5-INCH LOAF

2 cups all-purpose flour
2¹/2 teaspoons baking powder
¹/2 teaspoon baking soda
1 teaspoon salt
1 teaspoon cinnamon
¹/2 teaspoon nutmeg
1 cup light brown sugar
¹/2 cup (1 stick) butter at room
   temperature

1 cup pureed pumpkin
2 large eggs
¹/2 cup buttermilk
1 cup pecans, coarsely broken into
   medium-size pieces
¹/2 cup chopped dates *opt.*
   ? raisins

1. Preheat oven to 350°. Grease a 9- by 5- by 3-inch loaf pan. Line bottom and sides with wax paper and grease paper.

2. Sift together the flour, baking powder, baking soda, salt, cinnamon, and nutmeg, and set aside.

3. In a large bowl, beat brown sugar and butter until fluffy. Mix in pumpkin, eggs, and buttermilk, and beat until smooth.

4. Stir in flour mixture and beat only until smooth and flour incorporated.

5. Stir in nuts and dates.

6. Turn into prepared pan, and bake for 55 minutes to 1 hour or until a cake tester inserted in the middle comes out dry.

7. Cool on a rack for about 10 minutes. Cover pan with a rack and invert. Remove pan and peel off paper. Cover with another rack and invert again. Cool right side up.

⊠ Popovers

To be at their best, popovers should be eaten hot out of the oven.
When my mother made them for her brood, we gathered around
the stove and were likely to devour them before they reached the
table. My brothers liked theirs slathered with lots of home-churned
butter. I liked mine with jam.

MAKES 8 POPOVERS

2 large eggs at room temperature
1 scant cup all-purpose flour, sifted
1¹/₂ teaspoons salt

1 cup low-fat milk
2 tablespoons melted butter

1. Preheat oven to 450°. Butter 8 medium-size custard cups
and heat in oven for 4 or 5 minutes.
2. Place eggs in medium-size bowl and beat lightly with a whisk.
3. Beat in flour and salt. Stir in milk, using a wooden spoon.
Add melted butter and blend to make a smooth batter. Do not
overbeat.
4. Stir batter thoroughly from the bottom. Fill the custard cups
²/₃ full and place on a cookie sheet. Bake 25 minutes.
5. Lower the oven temperature to 375° and bake 20 minutes
longer. Do not open oven door until popovers are finished baking.
Serve at once.

⊠ Blueberry Sour Cream Scones

Traditional at English teatime are scones, a not-too-sweet small cake studded with currants or raisins and served with butter and marmalade or jam. Here is my version, made with fresh blueberries and sour cream.

MAKES 24 TRIANGLES

2 cups all-purpose flour
2½ teaspoons baking powder
½ teaspoon baking soda
1 tablespoon sugar
pinch of salt
4 tablespoons (½ stick) butter

½ cup sour cream
2 eggs, lightly beaten
1 teaspoon pure vanilla extract
1 cup fresh blueberries
confectioner's sugar

1. Preheat oven to 400°. Lightly butter a cookie sheet, or better still, line it with baking parchment paper.

2. Sift and mix flour, baking powder, baking soda, sugar, and salt in a bowl.

3. Cut butter into small pieces, and with your fingertips or pastry blender work butter into flour until mixture resembles coarse meal.

4. In a small bowl, mix together sour cream, beaten eggs, and vanilla extract, and stir until blended. Add to flour and butter mixture and blend.

5. Turn out on a lightly floured surface, knead lightly for half a minute, adding a little flour if dough is sticky.

6. Incorporate blueberries into dough gently, using your fingers.

7. Divide dough into 4 parts. Pat each into a circle, leaving dough ¾ to 1 inch thick. Cut each circle into 6 pie-shaped wedges and place on prepared cookie sheet, leaving a little space between.

8. Bake for 12 to 15 minutes until nicely browned.

9. Remove from baking pan and cool on rack. When cool, dust with confectioner's sugar. Store in a covered tin box.

◫ Ma Bert's Yeast Rolls

Ma Bert was — and is — a staunch family friend in North Caro-lina. She bakes and cooks professionally and is celebrated for a number of culinary triumphs, among them her Parker House–type dinner rolls. They freeze beautifully.

MAKES 5 TO 6 DOZEN ROLLS,
DEPENDING ON SIZE

1 package dry yeast
1 tablespoon sugar
1/3 cup warm water
3 eggs, beaten
1/2 cup vegetable oil

1/3 cup milk
1 teaspoon salt
3 1/4 cups all-purpose flour
melted butter

1. Dissolve yeast and 1 teaspoon sugar in warm water and stir well. Let stand 5 minutes or until bubbly.
2. Combine remaining sugar, eggs, oil, milk, and salt in a large mixing bowl. Stir until sugar and salt are dissolved.
3. Add yeast mixture and stir well.
4. Stir in enough flour, adding it a cup at a time, to make a soft dough.
5. Place dough in a greased bowl, turning dough so that all surfaces are greased. Cover with a kitchen towel and let rise in a warm place, free from drafts, for 1 hour, or until doubled in bulk.
6. When doubled, punch down dough and let rise 5 minutes.
7. Preheat oven to 450°. Grease a large baking sheet.
8. Divide dough in two and roll each portion on a lightly floured surface. Cut out circles of dough with a biscuit cutter and fold each circle in half. Place on baking sheet.
9. Bake for 12 minutes or until lightly browned.
10. Brush tops of rolls with melted butter, using a pastry brush. Serve warm.

Birthdays

◫ Birthdays were very special in my mother's home, almost surpassing Christmas since the glittering star of the occasion was one of the Hovis children instead of the old boy in the red suit and white beard. How the birthday child was coddled and indulged on his natal day! No household chores. No oatmeal. Lots of bacon. The celebrant chose the menus for the day and sat at the head of the table.

The holiday spirit made itself felt even at breakfast. My mother replaced the printed oilcloth that generally covered the kitchen table with a pretty linen tablecloth and added a centerpiece of whatever flowers were growing in our garden or nearby fields. My birthday breakfast menu never varied. I can still savor the hot fried pies my mother produced in my honor — flaky rounds of rich pastry folded into half-moon shapes, encasing a filling of juicy apple chunks oozing with fruity sweetness. I washed down countless fried pies with an orange drink, which had better be nameless since I think it is still being produced and there are libel laws. The drink was a glowing deep orange color that bore no resemblance to anything ever produced in nature. I found it bliss. No one in the family shared my enthusiasm for it, and it was not allowed in the house except on my birthday. I tasted it some years later when my palate had sharpened a bit and I found it horrendous — a sickeningly sweet liquid with fizz. So much for childhood illusions.

The birthday dinner was served in the dining room, a room ordinarily reserved for special occasions like holidays or Sunday dinner when the preacher was present. My dinner order was as predictable as my breakfast — fried chicken, hot yeast rolls, baked macaroni and cheese, Harvard beets, and, of course, the revolting orange stuff. The dinner came to a smashing crescendo with my mother's pound cake and hand-churned ice cream.

My birthday falls on July 7, which generally turns out to be the hottest day of the year, but I don't suppose it ever occurred to my mother that she had been "slaving over a hot stove." Air-conditioning in those days was unknown, but we had a splendid substitute that served the same purpose. In a vase were a large number of cardboard, wooden-handled fans. On one side was a picture with a religious motif and on the other, "Noble and Kelsey

Funeral Home." Mr. Kelsey was a close family friend who saw to it that we did not run out of fans.

I almost forgot to mention that there were never any gifts. Money was not plentiful, but good food, joy, and a spirit of loving and caring were, and not for a moment were we ever aware of the absence of gifts. Come to think of it, it is a tradition I continue. To this day, I find myself observing my friends' birthdays by cooking their favorite dishes in place of the more conventional store-bought presents.

Desserts

Cakes and Cookies

▧ Brown Sugar Coffee Cake

A promised visit from Granny Dameron's inner circle — the Misses Oresta, Dulcina, and Elmina — would invariably elicit this delight of a cake.

MAKES 1 10-INCH CAKE

CRUMB COATING
1 cup finely chopped pecans
¹/₄ cup light brown sugar
1 tablespoon cinnamon

CAKE
1 cup (2 sticks) butter at room temperature
2 cups granulated sugar
2 large eggs
1 cup sour cream

2¹/₄ cups cake flour (not self-rising)
1¹/₂ teaspoons baking powder
¹/₂ teaspoon baking soda
1 tablespoon grated orange rind
1 teaspoon vanilla extract

1. Preheat oven to 350°. Generously grease a 10-inch bundt pan.

2. In a small bowl, combine the chopped pecans, brown sugar, and cinnamon. Sprinkle half the mixture over sides and bottom of the bundt pan, twirling the pan and patting with your fingers to distribute evenly. Set aside.

3. In a large mixing bowl, cream butter and sugar until light and fluffy.

4. Add eggs one at a time, beating after each addition.

5. Beat in sour cream and blend well.

6. Sift cake flour, baking powder, and baking soda. Fold into batter, beating only until smooth.

7. Blend in orange rind and vanilla extract.

8. Transfer half the batter into bundt pan and sprinkle with remainder of sugar-nut mixture. Cover with remaining batter.

9. Bake for 35 minutes or until a cake tester comes out dry. Cool on a cake rack for about 15 minutes. Invert pan on a cake platter and remove pan. Let cool completely.

▨ Glazed Apple Cake

A dense, fruity cake that stays moist and fresh.

1½ cups vegetable oil
2 cups granulated sugar
½ cup light brown sugar
1 teaspoon vanilla extract
3 large eggs at room temperature
3 cups cake flour (not self-rising)
1½ teaspoons baking soda
1 tablespoon cinnamon

1 teaspoon allspice
1 cup Golden Delicious apples, peeled
  and coarsely chopped
1 cup Granny Smith apples, peeled
  and coarsely chopped
1 cup McIntosh apples, peeled and
  coarsely chopped
1 cup coarsely chopped pecans

GLAZE
12-ounce jar apricot preserves
¼ cup (½ stick) butter
¼ cup calvados

1. Grease and lightly flour a 10-inch tube pan. Preheat oven to 350°.

2. In a large mixing bowl, combine oil and sugars and beat well. Mix in vanilla extract.

3. Add eggs one at a time, beating well between each addition.

4. Sift together flour, baking soda, cinnamon, and allspice.

5. Add flour mixture to egg-sugar mixture and blend thoroughly, but do not overbeat. This makes a stiff batter. (If you wish, you may blend it in a food processor, using the steel blade, with limited on-and-off motions.)

6. Mix in the chopped apples, distributing them evenly.

7. Scrape into the baking pan and bake for 1½ hours. Cool cake in the baking pan on a rack before removing from pan. Cut around sides of pan and center tube to loosen cake, and invert pan on round cake plate. Remove sides and bottom of pan.

8. For the glaze, combine apricot preserves and butter in a small, heavy-bottomed saucepan. Heat and stir until melted and blended. Remove from heat and stir in calvados. Strain glaze and pour over cake.

9. Store cake in airtight cake box.

⊠ Carrot Cake

2¹/₂ cups cake flour (not self-rising)
2 teaspoons baking powder
1 teaspoon baking soda
¹/₂ teaspoon salt
1 teaspoon cinnamon
1¹/₂ cups (3 sticks) butter at room
  temperature
2 cups superfine sugar

3 eggs
1 cup crushed pineapple, drained (reserve juice)
2¹/₂ cups finely grated carrots
¹/₂ cup chopped toasted almonds
1 tablespoon grated orange rind
1 teaspoon vanilla extract

1. Grease and lightly flour two 9-inch round cake pans. Pre-heat oven to 350°.

2. Sift together flour, baking powder, baking soda, salt, and cinnamon. Set aside.

3. In a large mixing bowl, cream butter and sugar until light and fluffy.

4. Add eggs one at a time, beating well between each addition.

5. In a small bowl, mix crushed drained pineapple and grated carrots. Add to egg-sugar mixture and beat until well blended.

6. Stir in nuts, orange rind, and vanilla extract.

7. Add flour mixture and stir only until it is incorporated. Do not overbeat.

8. Divide batter evenly between the two cake pans. Bake for 35 to 40 minutes or until the cake springs back when pressed lightly in the center.

9. Cool for a few minutes, then loosen from sides of pans and turn out onto a rack to cool.

10. When completely cool, trim layers if necessary. If you wish, you can split each layer in half horizontally, making four layers.

11. Sprinkle layers lightly with reserved pineapple juice.

12. Spread cream cheese frosting (page 184) between layers, and frost top and sides of cake.

Cream Cheese Frosting

4 tablespoons (½ stick) butter at room
   temperature
8 ounces cream cheese at room temperature

1 teaspoon grated orange rind
1 tablespoon (or more) orange juice
1 teaspoon vanilla extract
1 pound confectioner's sugar, sifted

1. Blend butter and cream cheese until completely smooth. Add orange rind, orange juice, and vanilla extract, and mix well.

2. Add sifted sugar and blend into the mixture, adding an additional teaspoon or so of orange juice if needed.

Note: Garnish cake with tiny carrot shapes formed from the icing (optional).

▨ Fruit Cake

Baking fruitcakes, hanging holly wreaths, and decorating the Christmas tree all shared equal billing in preparing for the holiday at Granny Dameron's home, and they all had to be done at the same time. "It takes the smell of pine and the aroma of Christmas baking to fill the house with the real Christmas spirit," she maintained. Brainwashed as I was, I, too, never start my Christmas fruitcake ahead of time, and I find it ages almost instantly.

MAKES 2 9- OR 10-INCH FRUITCAKES

FRUITS

1 cup chopped candied orange peel
1 cup chopped citrons
1 cup candied cherries, cut in half
1 cup chopped pitted dates
1 cup moist-dried pitted prunes

1 cup dark raisins
1 cup white raisins
½ cup sweet sherry
½ cup bourbon

Place all fruits in a glass or porcelain bowl with sherry and bourbon. Cover bowl and let stand overnight, unrefrigerated. Stir from time to time until the fruit has absorbed the liquor.

NUTS

1 cup pecans, halved or very coarsely cut

1 cup almonds, slivered, halved, or very coarsely cut

1 cup black walnuts, halved or very coarsely cut

1 cup chopped candied ginger

Toast nuts lightly in a 350° oven for 15 to 20 minutes. Mix with chopped ginger and set aside.

CAKE

3 cups cake flour

2 teaspoons baking powder

1 teaspoon baking soda

1 tablespoon cinnamon

1 teaspoon mace

1 teaspoon ground ginger

1 tablespoon allspice

1¼ cups (2½ sticks) butter

2 cups dark brown sugar

12 eggs

1 cup lemon juice

2 tablespoons grated lemon rind

2 tablespoons grated orange rind

2 tablespoons vanilla extract

1. All ingredients should be at room temperature. Grease two 9- or 10-inch tube pans. Line bottom and sides with wax paper and grease paper. Preheat oven to 275°.

2. Sift flour, baking powder, baking soda, cinnamon, mace, ginger, and allspice into a large bowl and set aside.

3. In a mixing bowl, cream butter and sugar until light and fluffy.

4. Add eggs, one at a time, beating well between each addition.

5. To flour mixture, add soaked fruits and nuts, and mix well to separate fruits so that they are evenly distributed in the flour. You might find it convenient to use your hands for this.

6. To the butter-egg mixture, add lemon juice, grated lemon and orange rinds, and vanilla extract and mix well.

7. Fold flour into mixture and mix only until blended.

8. Divide batter evenly between the two pans.

9. Bake for 3 hours or until cake springs back when lightly pressed and has begun to leave the sides of the pan. Remove from oven and let cool on a rack. Cut around sides to release the cakes.

10. When cool, turn upside down and remove pans. Peel off paper and turn cakes right side up to finish cooling.

1 cup apricot jam
1 cup brandy
1/4 cup (1/2 stick) melted butter

Heat jam until melted. Combine with brandy and butter, and blend well. Brush tops of cakes with glaze while they are still warm.

To finish and store: Soak two large pieces of cheesecloth in about a cup of brandy and wrap cakes in soaked cheesecloth. Place in airtight containers with a peeled apple. Heavy aluminum foil may also be used to create an airtight covering. Cakes may then be placed in freezer bags and sealed. From time to time, you may add additional spirits if you like.

Any leftover cake will keep perfectly in the freezer until the next Yuletide.

⊠ Chocolate Fudge Cake Deluxe

Bake this cake at least two days before you plan to use it. It is a rich, dense cake that improves in flavor and texture on standing. It keeps fabulously well and gets better and better.

SERVES 12

6 squares unsweetened chocolate
6 tablespoons strong coffee
1 tablespoon pure vanilla extract
3/4 pound (3 sticks) butter or margarine at room temperature
1 pound dark brown sugar

1 cup granulated sugar
6 large eggs
1 cup sifted all-purpose flour
confectioner's sugar
1 cup heavy cream, whipped (optional)

1. Adjust rack in center of oven. Butter a 10-inch springform pan. Preheat oven to 350°.

2. Over simmering water, melt chocolate with coffee. When slightly cool, stir in vanilla. (The melted chocolate and coffee may form a thick paste, but it incorporates easily into the batter when added.)

3. In large bowl of electric mixer, cream butter or margarine with brown and white sugars until light and fluffy.

4. Separate eggs carefully, placing whites in a large bowl. Add egg yolks one at a time to butter-sugar mixture, beating well after each addition.

5. Add melted chocolate to batter and mix well. Stir in flour, mixing only until incorporated.

6. Using clean, dry beaters, beat egg whites until stiff and glossy but not dry.

7. Gently fold beaten egg whites into chocolate mixture, handling them carefully in order not to deflate the egg whites. Fold only until the whites disappear and no white streaks remain.

8. Gently turn the batter into the prepared springform pan. Smooth the top with a spatula. Place in preheated oven, and bake for 1 hour or until top springs back when lightly touched.

9. Remove pan from oven and cover top of cake with aluminum foil to keep the top from hardening. Place pan on rack to cool.

10. When completely cool, store covered in the baking pan until ready to use. A plastic bag, tightly closed, provides excellent storage. Do not refrigerate.

11. At serving time, remove sides of springform and place cake on a 12-inch cake platter. Dust top of cake lightly with confectioner's sugar. Accompany with a bowl of unsweetened whipped cream and top each portion with a dollop of the cream.

▨ Devil's Food Cake with 7-Minute Boiled Icing

MAKES 1 9-INCH LAYER CAKE

3 squares of unsweetened chocolate
1 cup granulated sugar
1/2 cup light brown sugar, firmly
   packed
1/2 cup (1 stick) butter, slightly soft
3 large eggs
1 1/2 cups sifted cake flour (not self-
   rising)

2 teaspoons baking powder
1/2 teaspoon baking soda
1/4 teaspoon salt
3/4 cup milk
2 teaspoons vanilla extract

1. Preheat oven to 350°. Grease and lightly flour two 9-inch round cake pans. Have all ingredients at room temperature.

2. Melt chocolate over boiling water or a flame-control device to prevent scorching. Remove from heat and let cool.

3. In a large bowl, cream sugars and butter until light and fluffy.

4. Mix in melted chocolate.

5. Add eggs, one at a time, beating well between each addition.

6. Sift together all dry ingredients.

7. Add to chocolate mixture alternately with milk, in three steps.

8. Stir in vanilla.

9. Divide batter equally in the two cake pans. Bake for 30 to 35 minutes or until top springs back when touched.

10. Cool cakes in pans for about 5 minutes. Cover with plate or cookie sheet and invert. Remove pans. Cover again with plate and invert to finish cooling right side up.

11. Frost with 7-minute boiled icing (below).

7-Minute Boiled Icing

2 unbeaten egg whites
1 1/2 cups sugar

1 1/2 teaspoons light corn syrup
5 tablespoons cold water

1. Mix all ingredients in the top of a double boiler.

2. Fill bottom of double boiler with hot water and place over moderate heat.

3. Beat with a rotary beater or an electric mixer at high speed until mixture stands in high peaks when beater is withdrawn.

4. Frost cake at once. Cover top of bottom layer, cover with top layer, then frost top and sides.

▨ Leo's Apple Gingerbread Ring

SERVES 10

APPLE TOPPING
2/3 cup dark brown sugar, lightly
    packed
6 tablespoons butter

2 Granny Smith apples
1/2 teaspoon cinnamon

1. Grease a 4-cup ring mold.

2. Add brown sugar and butter to ring mold and heat over low heat, stirring, until butter is melted and sugar dissolved.

3. Peel and core apples. Cut into quarters and cut each quarter into 3 slices. Place apple slices in syrup on bottom of mold. Sprinkle with cinnamon.

GINGERBREAD BATTER

*½ cup (1 stick) butter at room
  temperature*
½ cup dark brown sugar
1 egg, lightly beaten
1½ cups all-purpose flour
1 teaspoon ground ginger

1 teaspoon cinnamon
½ teaspoon ground cloves
1 teaspoon baking soda
pinch of salt
½ cup molasses
½ cup boiling water

1. Preheat oven to 350°.

2. In a medium bowl, cream butter and sugar until fluffy.

3. Add egg and beat well.

4. Sift flour, ginger, cinnamon, cloves, baking soda, and salt, and set aside.

5. In a measuring cup, combine molasses and boiling water.

6. Add flour mixture alternately with molasses mixture to the creamed butter and sugar. Beat only until smooth.

7. Pour batter over apples in the baking ring, and bake for about 30 minutes or until a cake tester comes out dry and the cake shrinks a bit from the edges.

8. Remove baking ring from oven and lightly run spatula around the sides, loosening cake.

9. Invert cake on a serving platter and allow to cool for 15 minutes.

10. Lift off baking ring. Let rest until completely cooled.

11. To serve, fill center of ring with a bowl of unsweetened whipped cream or lemon sauce (page 163), or scoops of vanilla ice cream.

▩ Grand Marnier Cake

This was one of the first cakes that earned me a reputation for good baking. A moist, feathery, orange-flavored cake that is suitable as a dinner dessert or a snack-time treat, it keeps beautifully fresh at room temperature for a week in a tightly closed plastic bag or an airtight container.

SERVES 10 TO 12

1¹/₄ cups granulated sugar
¹/₂ pound (2 sticks) butter at room
    temperature
3 large eggs, separated
¹/₃ cup Grand Marnier
2¹/₂ cups cake flour (not self-rising)
1 teaspoon baking powder
1 teaspoon baking soda

1 cup sour cream
¹/₂ cup coarsely chopped nuts
2 tablespoons grated orange rind
1 tablespoon grated lemon rind
¹/₃ cup fresh orange juice
2 tablespoons sugar
confectioner's sugar

1. Grease a 9-inch tube pan. Line bottom with a circle of wax paper (with a hole in the center to accommodate the tube) and grease paper. Lightly dust bottom and sides with bread crumbs and tap to remove excess. Set aside. Preheat oven to 350°.

2. In a large bowl, cream 1 cup sugar with butter until light and fluffy.

3. Add egg yolks one at a time, and beat well. Mix in 1 table-spoon of Grand Marnier, reserving the rest.

4. Sift together cake flour, baking powder, and baking soda. Add to egg mixture alternately with sour cream in three steps, mixing only until flour is smoothly incorporated. Mix in nuts and grated orange and lemon rinds.

5. In a medium-size bowl, beat egg whites until soft peaks form. Slowly add remaining ¹/₄ cup sugar, and continue to beat until stiff and glossy but not dry. Gently fold beaten egg whites into batter until no white streaks remain.

6. Transfer batter into the prepared pan, and bake in pre-heated oven for 45 to 50 minutes or until a cake tester inserted in the center comes out dry.

7. While cake is baking, in a small saucepan combine the re-maining Grand Marnier, the orange juice, and 2 tablespoons sugar. Bring just under the boil and stir until the sugar is dissolved.

8. Remove cake pan to wire rack to cool. Prick top of cake all over with a fork and spoon half the Grand Marnier syrup over cake. Let cool in the pan for 1 hour before inverting the pan on a round platter to unmold. Lift off sides and top of pan. Peel off wax paper. Prick cake with a fork, and spoon over the remaining Grand Marnier syrup. Let cool completely before serving. Dust top lightly with confectioner's sugar.

▨ Lemon Sponge Roll

SERVES 8 TO 10

6 large eggs, at room temperature
1 cup granulated sugar

1 cup cake flour, sifted (not self-rising)
1 teaspoon lemon extract

1. Grease sides of 15½- by 10½- by 1-inch jelly roll pan. Line bottom with baking parchment paper. Preheat oven to 350°.
2. Break eggs into the top of a double boiler or a heatproof bowl placed over simmering (not boiling) water. Add the sugar and warm, stirring, until sugar is dissolved.
3. Transfer to the bowl of electric mixer and beat at high speed until mixture is light lemon-colored and very thick.
4. Fold in flour and lemon extract.
5. Turn into the prepared pan and spread gently with a rubber spatula to level.
6. Bake 20 minutes or until top springs back when lightly touched and sides come away from pan.
7. Sprinkle a cotton or linen tea towel lightly with granulated sugar.
8. When cake is done, invert onto the towel. Remove pan and peel off paper. Starting from the long side, quickly and gently roll cake and towel together. Place on a rack to cool. Refrigerate when completely cool.

LEMON CREAM FILLING

⅓ cup all-purpose flour
¾ cup sugar
3 large eggs
1 cup milk

juice and rind of 2 large lemons
1 cup heavy cream, whipped
confectioner's sugar and strawberries

1. In a heavy-bottomed, nonaluminum saucepan, combine flour and sugar.
2. Beat in eggs, milk, lemon juice, and lemon rind.
3. Cook over medium heat, stirring constantly with a wooden spoon or spatula, until custard thickens and comes to a boil. Pour into a bowl and cover top closely with plastic wrap to prevent a skin from forming. Refrigerate until cold.
4. When chilled, fold in whipped cream.
5. Unroll sponge roll and spread top with filling. Reroll and place on a long platter, seam side down. Refrigerate.

6. Before serving, sprinkle with confectioner's sugar and surround roll with a border of sliced strawberries.

⊠ Mother's Pound Cake

SERVES 10 OR MORE

TO PREPARE PAN
4 tablespoons (¹/₂ stick) soft butter
1 slice white bread, crusts removed,
 made into fine crumbs in blender

BATTER
1 cup (2 sticks) butter at room
 temperature
2 cups granulated sugar
2 cups cake flour (not self-rising)
2 teaspoons baking powder

5 large eggs
¹/₂ cup buttermilk
1 tablespoon grated lemon rind
1 tablespoon lemon juice
1 teaspoon vanilla extract

SIMPLE SYRUP
¹/₃ cup sugar
¹/₃ cup lemon juice

¹/₃ cup water
3 tablespoons grated lemon rind

1. All ingredients should be at room temperature. Grease a 10-inch tube pan with soft butter and sprinkle bottom and sides evenly with bread crumbs, tapping out the excess. Set aside. Preheat oven to 350°.

2. In a large mixing bowl, cream butter and sugar until light and fluffy.

3. Sift flour and baking powder, and set aside.

4. Add eggs, one at a time, to butter-sugar mixture, beating well between each addition.

5. Add flour mixture alternately with buttermilk in three steps, ending with flour.

6. Mix in lemon rind, lemon juice, and vanilla extract.

7. Transfer to the prepared pan and bake for 1 hour or until top springs back when lightly pressed.

8. While cake is baking, prepare syrup. In a small saucepan, combine sugar, lemon juice, water, and grated rind. Bring just to a boil until sugar is dissolved.

9. When cake is done, remove from oven and let cool in the pan on a rack for 15 minutes.

10. Cover the pan with a rack, turn the pan and rack over, and remove the pan. Cover with another rack and carefully invert again to finish cooling right side up.

11. Brush top and sides with lemon syrup.

⊠ Strawberry Shortcake

MAKES 6 TO 8 SERVINGS

BISCUITS

2½ cups all-purpose flour
2 tablespoons baking powder
2 tablespoons sugar
12 tablespoons (1½ sticks) butter, cut into small pieces

1 cup sour cream
2 large eggs
1 teaspoon vanilla extract

TO ASSEMBLE

4 pints strawberries
2 tablespoons fresh lemon juice

½ cup superfine sugar
2 cups heavy cream, whipped

1. Preheat oven to 450°.

2. Combine flour, baking powder, and sugar in a sifter. Sift mixture into a mixing bowl.

3. Add butter and work with the fingers until well blended. Make a well in the center and add sour cream, eggs, and vanilla.

4. Blend well with the fingers. Turn dough out on a lightly floured surface and knead briefly.

5. Roll dough out on a lightly floured surface into a circle about 12 inches in diameter and about ½ inch thick. Using a biscuit cutter that is about 3 to 3½ inches in diameter, cut dough into rounds. As rounds are cut, arrange them on an ungreased baking sheet 1 inch or so apart. Gather up the leftover scraps of dough and roll out. Continue rolling and cutting until all the dough is used. There should be 12 or more rounds.

6. Place in the oven and bake 15 minutes.

7. Meanwhile, pick over the strawberries. Select 12 to 16 perfect, unhulled berries and set aside. Remove and discard the stems from the remaining berries and cut berries in half. There should be about 4½ cups. Place berries in a bowl.

8. Sprinkle berries with lemon juice and sugar, and blend well. Cover and refrigerate.

9. Split the biscuits in half. Arrange lower halves on a serving dish, split side up.

10. Whip cream until it stands in firm peaks. Using a pastry bag and star tip, pipe stars of whipped cream around the inside rim of each biscuit half. Fill the inside of the ring with sweetened strawberry halves.

11. Top each serving with the remaining biscuit half. Pipe whipped cream around the inside rim of each. Fill the centers with more of the sweetened strawberries. Garnish each serving with the reserved whole unhulled strawberries.

⊠ Crescent Cookies

A lovely cookie with afternoon tea or coffee. Accompanied by a glass of milk, they were a favorite childhood after-school snack offered by my mother in the hope of providing us with the energy we needed to attack our homework. After I came to New York, I recognized them as a southern version of a confection known in these parts as *rugelach,* a cinnamon-nut horn that may be of Hungarian origin.

MAKES ABOUT 4 DOZEN

PASTRY

1 cup (2 sticks) butter at room temperature
8 ounces cream cheese at room temperature

2 cups sifted all-purpose flour
pinch of salt

FILLING

1 cup chopped pecans
1 tablespoon grated orange rind
1/3 cup granulated sugar

1/3 cup light brown sugar
1 teaspoon ground cinnamon
confectioner's sugar

1. Cream together softened butter and cream cheese. Stir in sifted flour and pinch of salt, and work together to form a dough.

2. Form into individual balls, about the size of a walnut. Cover with plastic wrap and refrigerate overnight.

3. When ready to bake, preheat oven to 350°.

4. Mix together chopped nuts, orange rind, white and brown sugars, and cinnamon.

5. On a lightly floured surface, roll out each ball of dough into a circle 3 inches in diameter and about ⅛ inch thick.

6. Place a teaspoon of nut mixture on the upper half of each circle and fold over lower half, making a half-moon shape. Pinch outside edges together to make a firm seal. Turn the ends down slightly to form a crescent.

7. Place on lightly greased baking sheet (vegetable cooking spray works well) and refrigerate for 1 hour.

8. Bake in 350° oven for 12 to 15 minutes or until golden.

9. Remove from oven and sprinkle lightly with confectioner's sugar.

⊠ Lemon Butter Squares

Keep these in mind for your next occasion that calls for rich, buttery little tea cakes. This recipe makes a large quantity, but they freeze well.

MAKES ABOUT 60, DEPENDING ON SIZE

CRUST
2 cups all-purpose flour
½ cup sifted confectioner's sugar

1 cup (2 sticks) butter cut into small pieces

1. With the metal blade of the food processor in place, add flour, sugar, and butter to the container. Process with a few on-and-off turns until combined and a ball of dough forms on the blades.

2. Wrap dough in plastic wrap and refrigerate for 1 hour or place in freezer for 20 minutes.

3. Preheat oven to 350°. Butter a 10- by 15-inch jelly roll pan.

4. Pat the dough evenly over bottom of the pan.

5. Bake for 20 minutes and remove from oven. Let cool while you prepare the filling.

FILLING

4 eggs at room temperature
2 cups superfine sugar
6 tablespoons cake flour (not self-rising)
1 teaspoon baking powder

6 tablespoons fresh lemon juice
grated rind of 2 lemons
1 to 2 tablespoons confectioner's sugar

1. In a large bowl, beat eggs with an electric beater until they become thick and light-colored. Beat in sugar. Add flour mixed with baking powder, lemon juice, and grated rind, and blend well.

2. Pour mixture over baked crust and return to 350° oven. Bake for 20 minutes longer or until topping is set and golden.

3. When cool, sprinkle lightly with confectioner's sugar and cut into squares or oblongs.

▨ Orange Butter Cookies

Simple to make and delicious. A great favorite.

MAKES ABOUT 6 DOZEN

1 cup (2 sticks) lightly salted butter at room temperature
3/4 cup confectioner's sugar, sifted
2 tablespoons grated orange rind

1 tablespoon vanilla extract
1 tablespoon Grand Marnier
2 cups sifted all-purpose flour
2 cups bran flakes, crushed

1. Preheat oven to 375°. Grease a cookie sheet.

2. Cream butter and sugar until light and fluffy.

3. Mix in grated orange rind, vanilla extract, and Grand Marnier.

4. In a separate bowl, mix together sifted flour and crushed bran flakes. Add to butter mixture, blending with your fingertips.

5. Shape cookie batter into small balls, about 1/2 inch in diameter. Place well apart on cookie sheet and flatten each with the tines of a fork dipped in cold water.

6. Bake until lightly brown around the edges, 8 to 10 minutes. Cool before storing in airtight tin.

⊠ Pecan-Date Rolled Cookies

An easy-to-make cookie that stores well.

FILLING

1 pound pitted dates, finely chopped
1 tablespoon grated orange rind
1 tablespoon finely grated or ground candied ginger

⅓ cup sugar
½ cup orange juice
1 cup coarsely chopped pecans

COOKIE DOUGH

1 cup (2 sticks) soft butter
1 pound dark brown sugar
3 large eggs, lightly beaten
1 teaspoon vanilla extract

5 cups cake flour (not self-rising)
1 teaspoon baking powder
1 teaspoon ground ginger

1. Combine dates, grated orange rind, ginger, sugar, and orange juice in a small saucepan. Stir over moderate heat until mixture is blended and thick. Set aside to cool. When cool, stir in pecans.

2. In a large mixing bowl, cream butter and sugar until light and fluffy. Stir in beaten eggs and beat for 3 to 4 minutes. Beat in vanilla extract.

3. Sift together flour, baking powder, and ginger.

4. Add dry ingredients to egg-sugar mixture to make a soft dough. Wrap dough in wax paper or plastic and chill for 10 to 15 minutes.

5. Remove dough from refrigerator and divide in half. On a lightly floured surface, roll out dough into a 10- by 16-inch rectangle. Spread half of the date-nut mixture evenly over the top. Roll jelly roll fashion, beginning at the long end.

6. Repeat with remainder of dough and filling.

7. Wrap rolls in wax paper or plastic and refrigerate overnight.

8. Preheat oven to 350°. Line a baking sheet with parchment baking paper.

9. Cut the rolls into slices ⅓ inch thick and place cut sides up on baking sheet, leaving space between each cookie. Bake for 12 to 15 minutes, or until cookies are delicately browned. Remove from baking sheet and cool on a rack before storing.

⊠ Pecan Wafers

A delicate snack cookie to accompany a fruit dessert or a cup of afternoon tea.

MAKES ABOUT 4 DOZEN

1/2 cup (1 stick) soft butter
1 cup light brown sugar
1 egg, lightly beaten
1 cup sifted cake flour (not self-rising)

1 teaspoon ground cinnamon
1 teaspoon cocoa
1/2 teaspoon baking soda
1/2 cup coarsely chopped pecans

1. Preheat oven to 300°. Line a baking sheet with parchment baking paper.
2. In a medium-size electric mixing bowl, combine butter and light brown sugar and beat until creamy. Add beaten egg and continue to beat 3 or 4 minutes longer.
3. Sift together flour, cinnamon, cocoa, and baking soda. Stir into butter-sugar mixture and blend well.
4. Stir in chopped pecans.
5. Drop batter by level teaspoonsful on prepared baking sheet, leaving 2 inches between each cookie. (The cookies will spread as they bake and crisp as they cool.) Bake 13 to 15 minutes or until edges are lightly browned.
6. Remove cookies from baking sheet and let cool completely on a rack before storing in an airtight container.

Pies and Tarts

⊠ Upside-down Apple Pie

This is my mother's apple pie — juicy apple slices resting on a buttery flaky crust. And you can be sure that the crust will be flaky, since it is baked on *top* of the pie, which is then inverted, and thus escapes the soggy bottom crust syndrome that affects many fruit pies.

Serve the pie shortly after baking, when it will be at its best; it is not at its peak the next day.

SERVES 12

CRUST

1 tablespoon sugar

2 cups all-purpose flour, sifted

1/2 pound (2 sticks) chilled butter, cut
　　into small pieces

5 to 6 tablespoons ice-cold water

FILLING

1/4 pound (1 stick) melted butter

1 cup dark brown sugar, firmly
　　packed

1 tablespoon grated lemon rind

2 teaspoons cornstarch or arrowroot

5 or 6 tart apples, such as Granny
　　Smiths (about 2 pounds)

2 tablespoons bourbon

1. Place sugar, flour, and butter in a mixing bowl. Work them together with a pastry blender or your fingertips — I prefer the latter — until blended.

2. Gradually sprinkle mixture with ice-cold water, using only enough to hold dough together so that it can be patted into a ball. (This can also be done in your food processor: about 30 seconds on and off. Do not overprocess.) Shape dough into a ball and flatten. Wrap tightly with plastic wrap and refrigerate until ready to use.

3. Pour melted butter into a pie dish 12 inches in diameter and about 1½ to 2 inches deep, or the equivalent size in a rectangular dish. Add brown sugar and mix well with melted butter until completely incorporated. Spread mixture evenly over the bottom of the pie dish. Sprinkle with grated lemon rind and cornstarch or arrowroot.

4. Peel apples and cut away blemishes. Quarter apples and remove cores. Divide the quarters lengthwise in half. Arrange apple slices on their sides in neat concentric circles over brown sugar mixture. If there are any gaps between apple slices, you can fill them in with small pieces of chopped apples.

5. Allow dough to soften a bit at room temperature. Roll it out on a lightly floured surface into a circle about 13 inches in diameter and about ¼ inch thick. Carefully place the dough over the apples and fold over the overhanging dough toward the center, pressing lightly all around the outer rim so that apples are completely covered with dough.

6. Cover tightly with plastic wrap and refrigerate until ready to bake.

7. Preheat oven to 400°.

8. Place the pie on a cookie sheet or foil pan to catch the drips.

Bake for 50 minutes to 1 hour or until the crust is golden. Remove to a rack and cool for 10 minutes.

9. Run a knife around the outer rim of the pie to facilitate removal. Place a large serving dish over the pie and quickly invert the pie onto the serving dish.

10. Serve hot, warm, or at room temperature, but not chilled. Accompany with unsweetened whipped cream or ice cream, or you may glaze the top if you wish. Melt the contents of a small jar of apricot preserves over low heat until liquid. Strain and spread over the surface of the baked pie.

⊠ Apple Crumb Tart

SERVES 8 TO 10

CRUST

¹/₂ cup (1 stick) soft butter
¹/₃ cup sugar

1 cup all-purpose flour
¹/₂ teaspoon vanilla

1. Preheat oven to 425°. Grease a 9-inch springform pan.
2. In a small bowl, blend together butter and sugar. Mix in flour and vanilla until a soft ball forms.
3. Pat dough over bottom and halfway up the sides of spring-form pan.
4. Bake for 10 minutes. Remove from oven and let cool.

FILLING

*3¹/₂ cups Granny Smith apples,
    peeled, cored, and thinly sliced*
¹/₃ cup sour cream
2 eggs, lightly beaten

³/₄ cup sugar
¹/₄ cup all-purpose flour
¹/₂ teaspoon cinnamon

TOPPING

*Sweet potato pie crumb topping
    (page 208)*

1. Reduce oven heat to 350°.
2. Fill pastry crust with sliced apples.
3. In a small bowl, blend sour cream, eggs, sugar, flour, and cinnamon. Spoon over apples.

4. Sprinkle top with crumb topping.

5. Bake for 40 to 45 minutes, until custard is set.

6. When cooled, remove sides of springform pan. Serve at room temperature.

⊠ Cheese Cake Gems

Crowned with a mound of flavored sour cream, these delicate miniature cheese cakes make a super dessert or teatime treat.

MAKES 36 CAKES

CRUST

1/2 cup graham cracker crumbs   *1 tablespoon granulated sugar*
1/4 cup finely chopped nuts   *2 tablespoons soft butter*

1. Generously butter and lightly flour small muffin tins 1½ inches in diameter. Chill well in the refrigerator until ready to use.

2. In a small bowl, combine graham cracker crumbs, nuts, sugar, and soft butter. Mix lightly with your fingertips until combined. Set aside.

FILLING

1½ pounds cream cheese   *1 tablespoon pure vanilla extract*
1 cup sugar   *juice and grated rind of 1 lemon*
3 large eggs

1. Cut the cheese into large chunks and place in food processor or blender container with sugar. Blend until smooth, 3 to 4 minutes.

2. Add eggs, vanilla extract, and juice and grated rind of lemon. Process or blend until completely smooth and creamy, 7 or 8 minutes longer. You will have about 4 cups.

TOPPING

1 cup sour cream   *1/2 teaspoon pure vanilla extract*
2 tablespoons granulated sugar   *1 tablespoon rum or brandy*

In a small bowl, combine all ingredients and mix well. Set aside.

1. Preheat oven to 350°.

2. Remove chilled muffin tins from refrigerator and place ½ teaspoon crust mixture into the bottom of each cup, pressing down lightly with your thumb.

3. Fill each cup to the top with cream cheese filling. Bake for 20 minutes.

4. Remove tins from oven and let cool for 3 or 4 minutes before adding the sour cream topping. Increase oven heat to 425°.

5. Mound a generous ½ teaspoon of the sour cream topping in the center of each cheese cake, leaving the outside rims of the cakes exposed.

6. Return muffin tins to oven, and bake about 5 minutes longer or until the outside edges are slightly browned here and there.

7. Remove tins from oven, place on rack, and cool for 30 minutes.

8. Remove cooled cakes carefully from tins and refrigerate. Allow to come to room temperature before serving.

⊠ Chocolate Brownie Pie

My mother and her friends would heap scorn on any church supper that failed to include a chocolate brownie pie topped with whipped cream. I have taken a small liberty with the original recipe and have added Kahlúa, a coffee-flavored liqueur, for extra flavor.

SERVES 6 TO 8

CHOCOLATE CRUMB CRUST
1½ cups fine chocolate crumbs
5 tablespoons melted butter
2 tablespoons brown or white sugar

FILLING
½ cup sifted all-purpose flour
1 cup tightly packed light brown
   sugar
2 large eggs, beaten
½ cup (1 stick) butter, melted
1 cup toasted pecans, coarsely
   chopped

1 cup semisweet chocolate morsels
1 teaspoon vanilla extract
⅓ cup Kahlúa
whipped cream

1. Grease a 9-inch round pie plate and set aside.

2. Prepare crumbs by rolling chocolate wafers between two sheets of wax paper or whir them in a blender or food processor until uniformly fine.

3. Place crumbs in a bowl and mix with melted butter and sugar.

4. Pat crumbs evenly and firmly over the sides and bottom of pie plate, and place in freezer for 15 to 20 minutes.

5. Preheat oven to 350°.

6. In a medium-size mixing bowl, mix together flour and sugar. Add beaten eggs and mix well.

7. Blend in cooled melted butter.

8. Mix in toasted pecans, chocolate morsels, vanilla extract, and Kahlúa.

9. Transfer to crumb crust and bake for 45 to 50 minutes or until set. Do not overbake.

10. Cool and serve with whipped cream.

⊠ Lemon Chess Pie

As native to the South as magnolia blossoms and honeysuckle vines, chess pie is to be found in many versions, with each household featuring its own. I've been told that it was named at a dinner party in one of the large plantation homes when the cook carried it into the dining room at dessert time. "What's the pie?" asked one of the guests. The cook, unprepared and at a loss for words, murmured "Jes' pie." Another guest with a mouthful of the delectable stuff boomed with delight, "Chess pie! Heavenly." The story will do until a better one comes along.

SERVES 8

CRUST
1/4 pound (1 stick) chilled butter
1 1/2 cups all-purpose flour

pinch of salt
3 to 4 tablespoons ice water

1. Cut butter into 1/4-inch cubes.

2. Mix flour and salt in a mixing bowl. Add butter and blend with your fingertips until the mixture resembles coarse meal.

3. Sprinkle with ice water, using only enough to make a dough,

mixing with your fingertips until mixture forms a ball. Don't over-blend.

4. Cover tightly with plastic wrap and refrigerate for 30 to 40 minutes.

5. Let dough come to room temperature and roll out on a lightly floured surface until it measures about 12 inches in diameter and is about ⅛ inch thick.

6. Ease dough into a 9- or 10-inch buttered pie plate and press gently into sides and bottom of pan, leaving a ‚1-inch overhang along outside rim. Turn the edge under to make a rim of double thickness. Flute or press rim with tines of a fork.

7. Refrigerate until needed.

FILLING

2 cups granulated sugar
1 tablespoon all-purpose flour
1 tablespoon ground cornmeal
4 eggs at room temperature
4 tablespoons (½ stick) butter, melted

¼ cup light cream
¼ cup fresh lemon juice
2 tablespoons grated lemon rind
unsweetened whipped cream

1. Preheat oven to 375°.

2. Sift sugar, flour, and cornmeal into a mixing bowl.

3. Add eggs, melted butter, cream, lemon juice, and lemon rind, and beat until well blended and smooth.

4. Pour into unbaked pie shell, and bake for 45 to 50 minutes, or until set. Let cool. Serve with whipped cream.

▨ Heavenly Lemon Curd Pie

Feather-light, tart, a joyous ending to a good dinner. For best results, make the pie the day before you plan to serve it. An overnight stay in the refrigerator gives the flavor time to mellow.

SERVES 8 TO 10

MERINGUE CRUST

4 egg whites at room temperature
  (reserve yolks)
½ teaspoon cream of tartar
¼ teaspoon salt
1 cup superfine sugar

1 teaspoon vanilla extract
1 teaspoon white vinegar
1 teaspoon lemon juice
1 teaspoon grated lemon rind

1. Spray the bottom and sides of a 10-inch round glass pie plate with vegetable cooking spray. Preheat oven to 275°.

2. Place egg whites in the large bowl of electric beater (without a trace of yolk, please). With clean, dry beaters, beat egg whites until foamy. Add cream of tartar and salt, and continue to beat until soft peaks form.

3. Slowly add sugar, about 2 tablespoons at a time, alternating with vanilla extract, vinegar, lemon juice, and grated rind. Continue to beat until meringue stands in stiff, glossy peaks.

4. Gently transfer meringue into the prepared pie plate. With the back of a large spoon, cover bottom and press the meringue high on the sides, creating a deep nest for the filling.

5. Place in preheated oven and bake for 1 hour. Turn off oven and let meringue remain for 30 minutes.

6. Leave the oven door ajar and let meringue remain until completely cool, about 30 minutes longer.

FILLING

8 egg yolks	1/2 cup all-purpose flour
3/4 cup superfine sugar	1/3 cup grated lemon rind
1/2 cup fresh lemon juice	2 cups heavy cream, whipped
1/2 cup water	chocolate curls or grated coconut

1. In a medium-size bowl, combine egg yolks, sugar, lemon juice, water, flour, and lemon rind, and beat vigorously with a wire whisk until thoroughly blended.

2. Place the mixture in top of double boiler. Cook over simmering (not boiling) water, stirring constantly, until mixture becomes the consistency of custard, 15 to 18 minutes.

3. Remove top of double boiler from heat. Taste for sweetness and beat in additional superfine sugar if desired. (I prefer it tart.)

4. Cover top of custard with plastic wrap to prevent formation of a skin and allow to cool.

5. Whip cream until soft peaks form.

6. When the filling is cool, pour half into meringue shell. Cover with half the whipped cream, the remainder of the filling, and for the top layer, the remaining whipped cream.

7. Garnish with chocolate curls or a sprinkling of grated coconut.

8. Refrigerate until serving time.

▨ A Peach of a Pie

The Piedmont section of North Carolina where I grew up abounded with fruit orchards, particularly peach, and we were especially fortunate in having our own orchard. It was a modest size, but from it came enough apples, peaches, grapes, and figs for an endless stream of fruit pies throughout the summer. By the time September rolled around when the pear tree was laden with fruit, we had eaten ourselves silly with fruit pies, so most of the pears ended up as preserves at the hands of my resourceful mother. And how good those preserves tasted on a slice of homemade buttered bread or hot toast when the temperature plummeted! (Any of the above-mentioned fruits can be substituted in the recipe that follows.)

SERVES 6 TO 8

CRUST

1¼ cups all-purpose flour, sifted
½ cup (1 stick) butter, cut into small pieces

2 tablespoons sour cream
2 tablespoons chopped almonds

1. Place flour and butter in workbowl of food processor with the steel blade in place. Process with quick on-and-off turns until mixture resembles fine cornmeal.
2. Add sour cream and process with on-and-off turns for a few seconds until a soft dough forms.
3. Remove dough and mix in chopped almonds.
4. Place dough in the center of an ungreased 9-inch round cake pan 1½ inches deep with a removable bottom. Pat dough evenly over bottom and sides of pan. Refrigerate for 30 minutes.
5. Preheat oven to 400°.
6. Bake 10 to 15 minutes or until light brown. Remove from oven and set aside to cool. (Don't be concerned if the sides shrink a bit.)

FILLING

8 ripe medium peaches (I prefer Elberta)
3 egg yolks
⅓ cup sour cream

⅔ cup sugar
¼ cup all-purpose flour
1 teaspoon almond extract

1. Preheat oven to 350°.
2. Plunge peaches for 1 minute into boiling water and imme-

diately place in cold water. Slip off skins. Cut peaches in half, remove pits, and cut into thick slices.

3. Arrange slices in cooled pie shell in concentric circles, slices overlapping.

4. In a small bowl, combine egg yolks, sour cream, sugar, flour, and almond extract, and mix well. Pour over peaches.

5. Bake until custard is set, 45 to 50 minutes.

GLAZE

1/2 cup apricot jam
1/3 cup melted butter
1/3 cup brandy

1/2 cup toasted almonds, crushed with
a rolling pin
1 cup heavy cream, whipped
(optional)

1. In a small saucepan, heat jam and butter until melted. Remove from heat and mix in brandy.

2. When pie is cool, remove sides of pan. Paint glaze over top of pie and sprinkle crushed almonds in a border around pie.

3. Serve with unsweetened whipped cream.

◪ Sweet Potato Pie ✳ ✳ ✳

SERVES 6 TO 8

CRUST

1 cup all-purpose flour
1/4 pound (1 stick) cold butter, cut
into small pieces

2 tablespoons finely chopped pecans
3 1/2 tablespoons ice water

1. Place flour, cut-up butter, and pecans in container of food processor. With metal blade in place, process, turning on and off rapidly, for about 10 seconds. Do not overwork.

2. Add ice water and process only until a ball of dough forms on the blades.

3. Remove ball of dough and flatten slightly. Wrap in plastic wrap and refrigerate for 30 minutes.

4. Remove from refrigerator and roll out dough on a lightly floured surface.

5. Fit dough without stretching into a 9-inch pie plate and refrigerate.

FILLING

2 cups cooked mashed sweet potatoes
(deep orange-colored preferred)
2 large eggs
1 tablespoon grated orange rind
1 teaspoon nutmeg
1 teaspoon cinnamon
1/2 teaspoon ginger
1/4 teaspoon allspice
1 14-ounce can sweetened condensed
milk
1/4 cup (1/2 stick) melted butter
1 teaspoon vanilla extract

Place all ingredients in a large bowl and mix thoroughly.

CRUMB TOPPING

1/4 cup light brown sugar
2 tablespoons all-purpose flour
3 tablespoons chopped pecans
1 tablespoon grated orange rind
3 tablespoons butter

Combine all ingredients and mix together with a fork or your fingertips until crumbly. Set aside.

TO ASSEMBLE

1. Preheat oven to 400°. Place oven rack in center of oven.
2. Remove pie shell from refrigerator. Carefully ladle in filling.
3. Sprinkle with topping.
4. Bake for 1 hour or until crust is browned and filling is set.
5. Remove from oven and cool.
6. Serve at room temperature with brandy-flavored whipped cream.

Puddings and Fruits

▨ Apple Charlotte with Apricot-Brandy Sauce

A treat of a dessert, especially on a chill wintry day. The apple flavors blend wonderfully with the tangy apricot sauce.

SERVES 8

butter, sugar, and fine bread crumbs
   to line baking dish
1 loaf sliced white bread
4 tablespoons 1/2 stick) soft butter
1/4 cup dark raisins
1/4 cup golden raisins
1/3 cup calvados

4 medium Granny Smith apples
4 medium McIntosh apples
1/3 cup water
1/2 cup sugar
1 tablespoon grated orange rind
3 large eggs
1/2 cup blanched, toasted almonds

1. Generously grease a charlotte mold or 2-quart soufflé dish. Sprinkle sugar and fine bread crumbs lightly over bottom and sides of mold, tapping out excess. Preheat oven to 300°.

2. Remove crusts from bread. Butter slices lightly. Place on a baking sheet and toast in a 300° oven until slightly dried. Process in workbowl of food processor briefly, only until coarse crumbs are formed. Set aside. Increase oven heat to 350°.

3. In a small bowl, soak raisins in calvados. Set aside.

4. Peel apples and chop coarsely. Place in a saucepan with water, sugar, and grated rind. Cook over moderate heat until barely tender, not mushy. Transfer to a bowl.

5. Add toasted bread crumbs and mix.

6. Separate eggs, placing egg whites in a medium-size mixing bowl.

7. Beat egg yolks until foamy. Fold into apple-bread crumb mixture.

8. Beat egg whites until stiff peaks form. Fold into apple mixture until no white streaks remain.

9. Gently fold in toasted almonds.

10. Scrape into the prepared mold and bake for 1 hour. Unmold onto a round platter and serve warm, covered with apricot-brandy sauce (below).

APRICOT-BRANDY SAUCE

1 cup dried apricots
1 cup water
1/3 cup sugar

12-ounce jar apricot preserves
1/4 cup brandy

1. Combine apricots and water in a small saucepan and cook until apricots begin to soften.

2. Add sugar and apricot preserves, and simmer until apricots are completely soft and preserves melted.

3. Transfer to workbowl of food processor, using the steel blade, and process until liquefied.

4. Transfer to mixing bowl and stir in brandy. If sauce is too thick, thin with orange juice.

▨ Deep Dish Apple Cobbler

An old-fashioned treat. My mother served it warm, topped with whipped cream or homemade vanilla ice cream. I preferred the latter. I still do.

SERVES 8 OR MORE

CRUST

½ pound (2 sticks) lightly salted butter

2 cups unbleached all-purpose flour
4 to 5 tablespoons ice water

1. Cut cold butter into small cubes and place in a medium-size mixing bowl.
2. Sift flour and add to butter.
3. Work with a pastry blender or fingertips until it resembles coarse cornmeal. (I don't mind leaving a few lumps of butter; they add to the flakiness of the pastry.)
4. Sprinkle with ice water, just enough to form a dough. Mix and quickly gather into a ball. Dust lightly with flour.
5. Flatten ball slightly and wrap tightly in plastic wrap or aluminum foil. Refrigerate for 30 minutes.

FILLING

12 medium-size Granny Smith apples
1 cup granulated sugar
1 tablespoon grated orange rind
¼ teaspoon allspice

1 teaspoon cinnamon
1 teaspoon nutmeg
½ cup flour
¼ pound (1 stick) butter, melted

1. Peel and core apples and cut into eighths.
2. In a large mixing bowl, combine remainder of ingredients and mix well.
3. Add apples and toss thoroughly.
4. Transfer to a greased oblong baking dish, 9 by 13 inches and 2 inches high. Spread apples evenly.
5. Remove pastry from refrigerator. On a lightly floured surface, roll out crust into an oblong large enough to cover baking

dish with an inch of overhang all around, and to a thickness of
¼ inch.

6. Cover apples with pastry, trim overhang evenly, and turn
excess dough under edges. Crimp edges to make a tight seal, and
cut a few air vents in pastry to create an escape hatch for the
steam. Refrigerate for 15 minutes.

7. Preheat oven to 400° while cobbler is chilling.

8. Place cobbler in preheated oven and bake for 1 hour until
crust is nicely browned. (Use a cookie sheet or aluminum foil
under the baking dish to protect oven from the drippings.)

9. Remove from oven and let rest for ½ hour before serving.

⊠ Apple Brown Betty

Served warm and doused with heavy cream, this was a favorite
winter dessert during my childhood. It makes me think of the
glass milk bottles deposited early each morning on my mother's
front porch, the contents crowned with a few inches of opaque
heavy cream that was frequently saved to bring extra dazzle to a
fine dessert — apple brown betty, for example. Need I add that
the calvados was not part of the original North Carolina version
of the pudding? That's my contribution.

For best results, make the pudding the day before and refrigerate overnight.

SERVES 6

5 cups McIntosh apples, peeled,
    cored, and thinly sliced
10 slices white bread
10 tablespoons (1¼ sticks) butter at
    room temperature
1 cup sugar

1 tablespoon cinnamon
1 teaspoon allspice
2 tablespoons grated orange rind
¼ cup calvados
1 cup heavy cream (optional)

1. Butter an 8- by 8-inch glass baking dish and sprinkle lightly
with sugar. Set aside.

2. Prepare apples and set aside.

3. Remove crusts from bread. Break bread into pieces and
place in blender or food processor with butter cut into small pieces.
Blend or process into buttered bread crumbs.

4. Blend crumbs with sugar, cinnamon, allspice, and grated orange rind.

5. Spread a thin layer of bread crumbs over bottom of baking dish. Cover with a layer of sliced apples and a layer of bread crumbs, and continue until all are used, ending with a layer of bread crumbs.

6. Sprinkle with calvados.

7. Place a sheet of wax paper over baking dish and place a weight on top. Refrigerate overnight.

8. Preheat oven to 350°.

9. Remove weight and wax paper from baking dish, and bake for 45 to 50 minutes or until browned and bubbly.

10. Serve warm with a pitcher of heavy cream.

▨ Mincemeat-Stuffed Baked Apples

A juicy baked apple can be a dessert mainstay during the cold winter months. Served warm with a dollop of whipped cream on top or heavy cream poured over, it brings a dinner to a satisfying end.

SERVES 6

6 medium-size Rome Beauty apples	1/4 cup lemon juice
3 tablespoons mincemeat	1 cup apple juice
1 teaspoon cinnamon	2 tablespoons butter
1/2 cup granulated sugar	heavy cream or unsweetened whipped cream

1. Preheat oven to 400°.

2. Core apples about two-thirds of the way down, leaving the bottom intact. Remove about 1 inch of peel from around the stem end.

3. Stuff apple cavities with mincemeat.

4. In a small saucepan, combine cinnamon, sugar, lemon juice, apple juice, and butter, and bring to a boil. Reduce heat and cook until sugar is dissolved.

5. Place apples in a baking pan and pour syrup over. Bake for 1 hour or until apples are tender but not mushy. Baste with syrup frequently.

6. Transfer baked apples to serving bowls and spoon sauce over each.

7. Serve with heavy cream or unsweetened whipped cream.

▧ Apricot-Raisin Bread Pudding

½ pound (2 sticks) butter
3 small loaves brioche bread
½ cup golden raisins
½ cup dark raisins
¼ cup cognac
13 egg yolks

3 cups half-and-half
1 cup heavy cream
¾ cup sugar
2 teaspoons vanilla extract
1½ teaspoons cinnamon

APRICOT GLAZE
2 12-ounce jars apricot jam
¼ cup cognac
¼ pound (1 stick) butter

1. Preheat oven to 400°.
2. Melt butter.
3. Remove crusts from bread and cut into ¼-inch slices.
4. With a pastry brush, brush both sides of bread with melted butter.
5. Place on cookie sheets and bake until golden. Turn slices so that both sides are evenly colored.
6. Soak raisins in cognac.
7. In a large bowl, beat egg yolks until well blended.
8. In a medium-size saucepan, heat half-and-half, cream, and sugar just to the boiling point. Cook over low heat and watch carefully.
9. Slowly beat cream mixture into egg yolks, a small amount at a time, until well blended. With a slotted spoon, skim off some of the foam. Beat in vanilla extract and cinnamon.
10. Grease a 9- by 14-inch baking dish. Cover bottom with a layer of toast, sprinkle with soaked raisins, and cover with remaining toast. Spoon sauce over all. Cover with a sheet of plastic wrap and a light weight, such as a baking pan, to keep the toast from floating. Let stand for 45 minutes.

11. Preheat oven to 325°.

12. Remove weight and plastic wrap. Place baking dish in a larger pan in the oven. Pour in boiling water to come halfway up the sides of the baking dish. Bake for 1 hour or until set.

13. While the pudding is baking, prepare the apricot glaze. In a saucepan, heat jam, cognac, and butter over moderate heat until melted and blended, stirring often.

14. When pudding is set, remove from oven and cover immediately with glaze. Serve warm.

▨ Banana Pudding

Banana pudding, a delicious mélange fashioned of a rich vanilla custard with sliced bananas and cookie crumbs, was a staple in most southern households. It was topped with either meringue or whipped cream. My preference is the whipped cream, although the meringue may be slightly less sinful.

SERVES 4 TO 6

4 egg yolks
1/2 cup granulated sugar
1/4 cup all-purpose flour
1 cup heavy cream
1 cup milk
1 tablespoon vanilla extract

36 vanilla wafers
4 to 5 large ripe bananas, sliced
whipped cream flavored with rum, or
   meringue made with 4 egg whites
   and 3 tablespoons granulated
   sugar

1. In a medium-size bowl, combine egg yolks and sugar. Beat with an electric beater until thick and light. Beat in flour. Set aside.

2. In a heavy-bottomed saucepan, combine cream and milk and bring just to the boiling point.

3. Very slowly, whisk egg yolk mixture into hot cream mixture. Cook over moderate heat, stirring constantly, until mixture is thick enough to coat the back of a spoon.

4. Immediately remove from the heat and transfer to a bowl. Place the bowl in a larger one containing cracked ice and stir to cool. Add vanilla extract.

5. Cover with plastic wrap and chill in refrigerator.

6. Crush vanilla wafers between two sheets of wax paper, using a rolling pin, or in the food processor.

7. To assemble pudding, place a layer of cookie crumbs over the bottom of a 1½-quart soufflé dish or glass bowl. Cover with a layer of sliced bananas and a layer of custard. Repeat with layers of cookie crumbs, bananas, and custard, ending with a layer of cookie crumbs, until all are used. Cover and refrigerate.

8. At serving time, cover top with rum-flavored whipped cream or with meringue. Spoon into individual dessert bowls.

⊠ Mother's Three-Berry Pudding

A summertime pudding made with strawberries, blackberries, and raspberries crowned with unsweetened whipped cream.

SERVES 6 TO 8

2 pints strawberries, hulled
2 pints blackberries
2 pints raspberries
½ cup water
2½ cups granulated sugar
1 teaspoon grated orange rind

1 teaspoon grated lemon rind
1 loaf homemade type bread, crusts removed
1 tablespoon arrowroot
1 cup heavy cream, whipped

1. In a medium-size saucepan, combine berries, water, sugar, and grated orange and lemon rinds. Bring to a boil, and boil for 15 to 20 minutes or until the fruit becomes syrupy.

2. Transfer to workbowl of food processor and blend until pureed. Strain through a fine mesh strainer to remove seeds. Measure 1½ cups of sauce and set aside for final glazing.

3. Grease a 1-quart soufflé dish. Line the bottom of the dish with a layer of bread, spoon sauce generously over bread, and continue layering until all the bread and sauce are used.

4. Place a sheet of wax paper over pudding and cover paper with a weight. Place the soufflé dish on a plate in case there is any overflow as the pudding rests. Refrigerate overnight.

5. Before serving, dissolve the arrowroot in the reserved 1½ cups of sauce. Heat over moderate heat with a minimum amount of stirring until the sauce is thickened and clear.

6. Unmold pudding on a platter and glaze with the thickened sauce.

7. Serve with unsweetened whipped cream.

⊠ Orange Slices in Champagne-Ginger Sauce

My good friends Peter Duchin and his wife, Brooke Hayward, generally reply to my dinner invitation with an order posed as a question: "Are you having those oranges?" Here are those oranges:

SERVES 6 TO 8

8 large navel oranges
1 cup ginger marmalade
1 cup stem ginger in syrup

½ cup superfine sugar
2 cups dry champagne
½ cup slivered almonds, toasted

1. Using a sharp knife, peel oranges, removing all of the white pith. Slice oranges into ¼-inch rounds. Place in a glass bowl.

2. In container of blender or food processor, with the steel blade in place, combine ginger marmalade, stem ginger, sugar, and champagne. (If you are using a large bottle, I suggest you consider drinking the rest.) Process until completely smooth.

3. Pour mixture over oranges, cover with plastic wrap, and refrigerate overnight. Turn the oranges occasionally.

4. Before serving, toast the almonds lightly. This may be done either in a 350° oven or on top of the stove with a scant teaspoon of oil, shaking the pan often. Sprinkle oranges with toasted almonds.

Fresh Pineapple Custard in Shells

SERVES 4 OR 5

1 large ripe pineapple
4 egg yolks
1/2 cup granulated sugar
1/4 cup all-purpose flour
1 cup milk

1 cup heavy cream
1 teaspoon vanilla extract
2 tablespoons Kirschwasser
8 macaroons, made into crumbs

APRICOT GLAZE
12-ounce jar apricot preserves
1/4 cup (1/2 stick) butter, melted
2 tablespoons Kirschwasser

1. Cut pineapple in half from top to bottom, so that each portion has half the plume. Carve out pineapple meat, discarding core, and cut into 1-inch cubes. Set aside.

2. In a medium-size bowl, combine egg yolks and sugar, and beat with an electric beater until light and thick. Beat in flour. Set aside.

3. In a heavy-bottomed saucepan, combine milk and cream, and over low heat bring just to the boiling point.

4. Very slowly, whisk egg yolk mixture into hot milk-cream mixture and cook over moderate heat, stirring constantly, until mixture is thick enough to coat the back of a spoon.

5. Immediately remove pan from heat and pour custard into a bowl that is placed in a larger bowl containing cracked ice. Add vanilla extract and Kirschwasser to custard, and stir until cool. Cover closely with plastic wrap and chill in refrigerator.

6. Crush macaroons between two sheets of wax paper, using a rolling pin, or process in food processor. Set aside.

7. Combine pineapple cubes and custard, and fill pineapple shells.

8. Top with apricot glaze and sprinkle with macaroon crumbs. To prepare the glaze, heat apricot preserves with butter and stir until melted. Remove from heat and stir in Kirschwasser. Strain glaze and cool.

▨ Poached Pears in Sauternes with Vanilla Sauce

SERVES 6

6 fine ripe pears
2 cups cold water with ¼ cup lemon
  juice
2 cups Sauternes
1¾ cups granulated sugar
peel of 1 medium orange, cut into
  strips

2 cinnamon sticks
1 vanilla bean
2 whole cloves
vanilla cream sauce (page 164)

1. Bosc pears are a good choice. With a swivel-bladed vegetable peeler, peel pears carefully, leaving the stems intact. Remove lower portion of the core and scrape bottom of pear so that it will stand erect. As the pears are peeled, drop them in a bowl of water and lemon juice to prevent darkening.

2. In a nonaluminum saucepan — enamel-lined or stainless steel — combine Sauternes, sugar, orange peel, cinnamon sticks, vanilla bean, and cloves. Bring to a boil, and boil until sugar is dissolved.

3. Add peeled pears, reduce heat, and poach uncovered until pears are tender. Time will vary, depending on size and ripeness of pears, 20 to 40 minutes or longer. Turn pears from time to time. Test for doneness with a knitting needle: when you can pierce the center of the pear without encountering resistance, consider it done.

4. Let pears cool in syrup. When cool, cover and refrigerate.

5. To serve, remove pears from liquid, transfer to a dessert bowl or large sherbet glass, and mask pear with vanilla cream sauce. Serve chilled.

▨ Fresh Stewed Rhubarb and Strawberries

Take advantage of the time when rhubarb is in season to make this simple and refreshing dessert.

SERVES 6

6 cups fresh rhubarb (about 1½
   pounds)
1 cup granulated sugar
1 cinnamon stick
1 tablespoon ground ginger

1 tablespoon grated orange rind
1 pint fresh strawberries
1 cup heavy cream, whipped
¼ cup sugar

1. Wash rhubarb, and trim off root and leaf ends. Peel if it has coarse strings. Cut stalks into 2-inch pieces.

2. Mix sugar, cinnamon stick, ginger, and grated orange rind. Mix with rhubarb slices and refrigerate overnight, covered.

3. Preheat oven to 350°. Place rhubarb in a lightly greased, nonaluminum baking dish, such as stainless steel, enamel, or glass. Cover with aluminum foil and bake for 15 to 20 minutes or until rhubarb is fork-tender. Cool to room temperature and refrigerate.

4. To serve, place rhubarb in individual dessert bowls and garnish tops with sliced strawberries. Top with whipped cream sweetened with ¼ cup sugar.

⬚ Kirsch-flavored Strawberries

This always comes to mind when I come across those wonderfully large strawberries with stems in the market. The dessert requires little effort and makes a spectacular presentation.

SERVES 6

24 large strawberries, preferably with
   stems
2 egg whites
¼ cup Kirschwasser or strawberry
   vermouth

1 cup granulated sugar
1 cup unsweetened whipped cream
   flavored with 1 tablespoon Kirsch-
   wasser or strawberry vermouth

1. Gently wipe strawberries clean with a damp paper towel.

2. In a small bowl, mix egg whites with Kirschwasser or strawberry vermouth, but do not beat.

3. Place sugar in a shallow bowl or on a square of wax paper.

4. Dip the strawberries first in egg white mixture and then in sugar. Place sugar-coated berries on a wire rack and allow to dry, turning berries a few times and sprinkling lightly with additional sugar.

5. To serve, arrange berries on a round glass plate or silver tray around a small bowl of liqueur-flavored whipped cream, and allow the guests to do their own dipping.

VARIATION

Broiled Strawberries: Use 24 large strawberries, prepared as for the preceding Kirsch-flavored strawberries. Preheat broiler and lightly grease a baking sheet. Place sugar-coated berries in a single layer on baking sheet. Broil about 4 inches from the source of heat until sugar begins to caramelize. Turn berries and broil other side. Serve at once with a bowl of Kirschwasser-flavored unsweetened whipped cream.

⊠ Frozen Chocolate Mousse

I have a special affection for foods — particularly desserts — that can be prepared in advance. This is a splendid, no-cooking extravaganza that happily minds its own business in the freezer 24 hours ahead of when you are ready to serve it.

SERVES 10

6 large eggs
3 tablespoons instant espresso coffee
1/2 cup hot water
16 ounces semisweet chocolate morsels
1/2 cup granulated sugar
1/4 teaspoon salt

1 1/2 cups heavy cream
1 tablespoon vanilla extract
24 ladyfingers
1/4 cup dark rum
vanilla cream sauce (page 164)

1. Separate eggs, placing yolks and whites in two large mixing bowls. Set aside.
2. Dissolve espresso coffee in hot water and set aside.
3. Melt chocolate in the top of a double boiler over hot water, stirring until melted.
4. Mix chocolate with dissolved coffee and set aside to cool.
5. With electric beater at high speed, beat egg yolks about 3 minutes, until light lemon-colored. Slowly beat in sugar and beat about 5 minutes longer, until thick.
6. Slowly beat in cooled chocolate mixture and blend well.

7. With clean dry beaters, beat egg whites and salt until they are stiff but not dry and stand in firm peaks. Gently fold into chocolate mixture.

8. Beat heavy cream until soft peaks form. Fold into chocolate mixture.

9. Mix in vanilla extract.

10. Split ladyfingers and brush with rum. Line bottom and sides of 10-inch springform pan.

11. Turn chocolate mixture into springform pan and spread top gently with a rubber spatula to level.

12. Cover tightly with plastic wrap or aluminum foil and place in freezer. Remove from freezer to refrigerator ½ hour before serving.

13. To serve, place on a round platter. Remove plastic wrap or aluminum foil. Remove sides from springform pan. Serve with vanilla cream sauce.

⊠ Frozen Orange Pudding

A refreshing hot-weather dessert that combines the pleasures of ice cream, frozen custard, and a soufflé.

SERVES 10

8 egg yolks
¾ cup granulated sugar
½ cup fresh orange juice
grated rind of 3 oranges

¼ cup Grand Marnier
4 cups heavy cream, whipped
24 ladyfingers
3 tablespoons brandy

1. Separate eggs, placing yolks in a medium-size mixing bowl. (Save whites for another use.) Beat egg yolks until thick and light-colored.

2. In a heavy-bottomed saucepan, combine sugar, orange juice, and grated rind, and bring to a boil. Boil for 5 minutes.

3. Very slowly, add hot syrup to egg yolks, beating with an electric beater. Let mixture cool and beat in Grand Marnier.

4. Beat heavy cream until soft peaks form. Set aside ½ cup for garnish.

5. Lightly brush both sides of ladyfingers with brandy. Line sides and bottom of springform pan with ladyfingers. Split and break remainder and set aside.

6. Fold whipped cream into egg yolk mixture and blend thoroughly.

7. Pour about a third of the mixture into the springform pan. Distribute a few of the split and broken ladyfingers, and continue to layer, alternating custard and ladyfingers and ending with the custard mixture. Cover pan tightly with plastic wrap and place in freezer for several hours.

8. Remove from freezer to refrigerator about ½ hour before serving.

9. When ready to serve, remove sides from springform pan. Garnish top of pudding with whipped cream rosettes and shaved chocolate or a sprinkle of cocoa.

⊠ Strawberry Melba in Almond Cups

The first Melba to be immortalized in gastronomy was Nellie Melba, the famed diva. This dessert has nothing to do with operatic stars. It is named for my dear, longtime friend Melba Tolliver.

SERVES 6 TO 8

SAUCE

10-ounce package frozen raspberries, thawed
1 cup confectioner's sugar

1 tablespoon lemon juice
¼ cup Kirschwasser

1. With the steel blade in position in food processor, process all ingredients until liquefied.

2. Strain sauce through a fine mesh strainer to remove seeds.

3. Refrigerate in a covered container.

ALMOND CUPS

2/3 cup granulated sugar
1/2 cup all-purpose flour
1 whole egg at room temperature
2 egg whites
1 teaspoon vanilla

1/4 cup (1/2 stick) melted butter
1/2 cup sliced almonds
1 tablespoon light cream or half-and-half

1. In a medium-size mixing bowl, combine all ingredients and blend thoroughly. Allow batter to rest for 1 hour at room temperature.

2. Preheat oven to 400°. Line a baking sheet with baking parchment paper. Place rack in the center of the oven.

3. Place 1 tablespoon almond mixture on baking sheet. With a large spoon, spread to make an even round circle about 6 inches in diameter. Leave at least 1½ inches between each cookie. Continue until all the batter is used.

4. Bake for 8 to 10 minutes, or until just golden. Do not allow to brown.

5. Remove the baking sheet from the oven, leaving it on the open door of the oven to keep warm and soft while you form the cups. Work quickly, since the cookies harden quickly. To mold a cup, place a cookie over the top of a 2-inch cup or can and press sides down to form a cuff that will fan out a bit. This will make 6 to 8 cups in addition to a few that will inevitably be ruined — par for the course.

TO ASSEMBLE

2 pints strawberries
1 pint vanilla ice cream

1. Wash and hull strawberries, reserving 6 to 8 of the biggest and the best for garnish. Drain well.

2. Cut remainder of strawberries in half and mix with raspberry sauce.

3. Just before serving, place a scoop of vanilla ice cream in each cup. Spoon sauce over ice cream and top with a strawberry.

⊠ Fresh Peach Ice Cream

A taste treat for ice cream lovers.

12 ripe peaches
2 cups superfine sugar

½ cup fresh lemon juice
2 tablespoons grated lemon rind

CUSTARD
4 eggs
2 cups superfine sugar
6 cups half-and-half

2 cups heavy cream
2 tablespoons vanilla extract
½ teaspoon salt

1. Dip peaches in boiling water for 1 minute, then into cold. Slip off skins and cut peaches in quarters.
2. Place peaches in workbowl of food processor with the steel blade in place. Add sugar, lemon juice, and lemon rind. Process with a few on-and-off turns until pureed. You may have to do this in two batches.
3. In a large mixing bowl, beat eggs until light.
4. Add sugar and beat until mixture becomes very thick.
5. Add remaining ingredients and mix thoroughly.
6. Add peach puree and blend well.
7. Fill the freezer can (not more than three-quarters full, since space is needed for expansion) and proceed with the freezing according to manufacturer's directions.

Linen and Old Lace

⊠ I have always had a passion for tablecloths, napkins, place mats, and pillow shams that date from an era when there was time for delicate embroideries and fine seams with tiny running stitches. Over the years, I have found collecting almost as satisfying as ownership. I reveled in the challenge and unpredictability of sifting through bins of jumbled linens in thrift shops or coming upon a treasure at a country auction that was not only rare and beautiful but also cheap. It's a far cry from today, when antique linens are in vogue and are prized and priced accordingly by dealers in New York, London, and little antique shops tucked away in obscure, out-of-the-way hamlets. Few bargains these days.

Granny Dameron taught me to appreciate fine, handmade linens. I was fascinated by how she transformed undistinguished squares of cloth into wonderful table napkins with lovely cross-stitch designs or edgings of colorful embroidered flowers. I loved seeing an intricately crocheted lace border take shape around a large linen oblong, changing into a tablecloth fit for a banquet. When finished, all the pieces were starched to a fare-thee-well with good old Argo starch reinforced with sugar for more stiffening.

Household schedules in Granny Dameron's home were sacrosanct. Monday she washed and Tuesday she ironed, and nothing short of a natural disaster or a human catastrophe was allowed to interfere. She had a special way of laundering and tolerated no shortcuts. First she boiled the linens for about an hour in a big black wash pot, the same one that later doubled as a cook pot for the fish fries that produced the most spectacular porgies you ever tasted. After the boiling process that bathed the kitchen in clouds of swirling steam, she rinsed the linens in several changes of cold water. She dipped the ecru and deep cream-colored linens and laces in a solution of strong tea to restore the color and dried them in the shade to prevent fading.

The white linens, on the other hand, were dried in the sun so that they would be bleached to a pure, shining white — which reminds me of my little cousin whom we called "Snooks." On one occasion, Snooks stayed in the sun so long she became quite ill. As she explained it, her reason was valid. If the sun could turn linens white, why couldn't it do the same for a little dark-skinned girl? Poor Snooks. She had to learn the hard way that skin tones are permanently built in.

I was permitted to help with the ironing. I considered it a great privilege, even though I was restricted to small, flat pieces — napkins, handkerchiefs, and the like. The large intricate pieces were in Granny Dameron's domain.

The ironing process began with heating the heavy black irons on top of the stove, several at a time. I admired the way Granny Dameron moistened the tip of her right-hand index finger on her tongue and ever so lightly touched the finger to the iron. A slight, almost indiscernible hiss would announce that the iron was hot enough. She kept a watchful eye on my work — a stern taskmaster, my grandmother. "No cat faces," she would admonish if wrinkles appeared in my handiwork.

I still take care of my important linens. I find the act of ironing fine therapy for relieving tensions. There is something quieting about running a hot iron over a piece of linen and seeing the fabric emerge smooth and tranquil. And then comes the gratification of stacking the freshly laundered pieces in neat piles, creating a sense of order. I store my linens in a large antique armoire, fitted with shelves that slide out for easy access to the contents.

Following are my laundry techniques for fine linens. You will need a detergent, a powdered bleach, and spray starch. I sometimes treat individual stains on white linens with an application of Windex, which contains ammonia.

1. Wash linens by hand.

2. If the linens are stained with such things as lipstick, wine, or yellowing caused by age, boil a large amount of water. When it comes to a boil, add 3 tablespoons of powdered bleach. (I use Clorox 2 or Snowy Bleach.)

3. Place linens in the boiling water, and boil for 5 minutes.

4. Rinse linens thoroughly in cold water.

5. Wring out linens, extracting as much water as possible, and place in a plastic bag. Refrigerate until very cold.

6. Heat iron. Spray linens with spray starch and go to work. You will find the results rewarding.

Index